Watching Cricket on the Radio

Dr. Dan Diaper

Published by New Generation Publishing in 2015

First Edition

Cover Photograph: *Batting in the Mind's Eye.*
© 2015, Dr. Dan Diaper.
Un-retouched photograph taken from the television,
England v. India, August, 2011.

www.newgeneration-publishing.com

Dedications

Personal

To the bJw, the beautiful Japanese wife (a.k.a. Aki or Mrs. Atsuko Kawamura) for encouraging my "work" on this book and so letting me watch cricket for nearly every day of 2014.

Professional

To Martin Emmerson of BBC Radio Newcastle as my most appreciated cricket commentator in 2014, and especially for his "Dr. Dan voice".

To Geoffrey Boycott as the best technical cricket commentator. He has a brace of chapters.

An Hon. Mention to David Townsend (DT) who is technically nearly as good as Sir Geoffrey, and much funnier.

Table of Contents

Preface

Do people read book prefaces? I do. They should be useful, although, I fear, my academic colleagues often don't put in the effort I think a good preface deserves. You should read this one because it is designed to help and, allegedly, amuse you.

In charge of the BBC from its inception in 1922, 1st. Baron (John) Reith lent his name to the aims that public service broadcasting should "educate, inform and entertain". 'Watching Cricket on the Radio' is unashamedly Reithian, intending, with a little alliteration, to elevate, educate and entertain.

Having spent my working life as a scientist and research engineer, my technical publications have been short of any entertainment factor, the aim being precision and clarity of thought. Trust not writers' opinions of their own humorousness, yet I take comfort that it is impossible to sink below the standards set by the "alleged humorist" B. Henderson Asher who's 'Moments of Mirth', says Wodehouse's Psmith, "have frequently reconciled me to toothache" [1, p44]. Allegedly humorous cricket books aren't as bad as that, but, generally, the bar's not set so high that I could possibly limbo dance beneath it. A hint of humour, a douche of doubt, illuminating imaginings, serious science, and too much alliteration, are more my metier, although a few chapters do wonder and wander with whimsical notions: on the design of bowler's boots (Chapter 2); numerology and cricket scores (Chapter 12); a cloned cricketer (Chapter 22); and cricket playing primates (Chapter 25).

Notwithstanding whimsy, weird ideas and silly speculations, like a good woman behind every successful man, behind every chapter is a point or three of seriousness. I suppose I was a selfish scientist, I just wanted a better understanding of how stuff worked. To educate others, rather than myself, was always a secondary concern, but not one I ever neglected.

Why would I spend a year of my life writing this book? As a professional, albeit technical, author, I strongly disapprove of narcissist diarists who write for themselves. Most of my readers will be cricket followers, even cricket fans, and I can't get out of the habit of trying to educate 'em. I might not elevate them, a matter of morality I believe, but I trust that education and entertainment will suffice, or better, *vice versa*, that entertainment and a spoonful of education will do.

I'd also like to think that there may be a secondary, academic market for 'Watching Cricket on the Radio'. Not in the science, but in how science, engineering and design can be applied to prosaic, everyday things and here cricket is just the context used to characterise how technical knowledge can, and should, be applied, and often isn't outside of work contexts. As a pushy postgraduate in the Department of Experimental Psychology, University of Cambridge (1977-82), I was as a youth genuinely shocked when I'd regularly ask of the great and good who would visit Cambridge how being a psychologist changed their own everyday life. In almost every case the answer was "Not a lot." In contrast, I've always treated everything with the same seriousness, from making a cup of coffee, making love to my technical work, my mental attitudes and approaches are identical, and this certainly includes my more than a quarter of a century watching cricket on the radio (and occasionally on television).

Every chapter's a bit of a mixed bag, but most have a main theme and I've quite deliberately mixed them up so, if in the unfortunate, and I trust unusual, case where a chapter doesn't, as Psmith would like, really "grip" my reader, then the next one will be a little, if not completely, different. I've thrown in a few book reviews: about Kent County's history (Chapter 7); on a funny, in two senses, book (Chapter 11); I defend Geoffrey Boycott's latest autobiography (Chapter 18); and, to an extent, review Mike Brearley on captaincy (Chapter 21).

A lot of this book is about my own interest in cricket (Chapter 1), how I watch cricket on the radio (Chapter 4) and what I do to understand and gauge a cricket match's progress (Chapters 14 and 23), and what I'd like from a good game (Chapter 10). I've included three chapters that are about particular cricket matches I watched on the radio in 2014 (Chapters 3, 9 and 15).

Mostly completely complimentary about cricket commentators, I've a peeve (Chapter 6) and various more or less practical suggestions for commentary improvements (Chapters 13, 20 and 26) and about television advertising during matches (Chapter 24). My psychology and cricket commentary intersect (Chapters 8 and 27).

My psycholinguistics leads me from watching a game in Pakistan to speculation on English as the *de facto* global language (Chapter 17). Besotted by design, its theory and practice, I've written about modern television cricket technologies, of the snickometer (Chapter 5) and Hawkeye (Chapter 16), and about the design of cricket equipment, batsmen's pads particularly (Chapter 19).

There! I've counted and that's every chapter mentioned. It's just one categorisation (see Chapter 8) and I could redraft this preface and give my readers a radically different organisation of this book. One preface, however, is enough and two would be greatly greedy.

Watching cricket on the radio has occupied my life in 2014. I spent more than three hundred days in the year watching matches on radio, television or both. Most mornings I spent three or four hours writing 'Watching Cricket on the Radio'. I have enough notes to start writing the sequel immediately. I shall only start if there is any demand for another, and (logical AND) that this book has made at least a miniscule profit, professional author to the last that I am.

[1] Wodehouse, P.G. (1915) *Psmith Journalist*. Penguin.

Chapter 1

Why Cricket?

I was in my mid-thirties when I came to the conclusion that a well rounded human being should, at least, follow one sport. By the time I was old enough to vote at eighteen, I had abandoned sports as irrelevant ephemera. I still think I was right to do so; I had much more important and exciting things to learn. So, which one sport should I choose to follow?

At the time I was an atheist living in Liverpool, where the religion is football. The city has two cathedrals, one for red Liverpool FC and one for the blue, Everton team. Ancient joke: Q. 'What's the second best team in Liverpool?' A. 'Liverpool Reserves' or 'Tranmere Rovers'[1]. I'd played football at school, but I couldn't face being a neophyte in Liverpool's established religion.

I did consider athletics as while at school I'd been good at running, from 80 metres hurdles to cross country. Against choosing athletics is that it is lonely sport, an individual competing against themselves as much as against others. Thinking about this, I decided I'd prefer to follow a team sport.

Not rugby! Only one of the four grammar schools I attended when aged between 11 and 16 forced me to play rugby. All I remember of that one miserable sporting winter was stud marks on my little, prepubescent chest and a rational desire, if by disaster I found the ball in my hands, to get rid of it immediately, into touch for the sake of team

---

[1] For Tranmere, cross the Mersey to its south side to God's Hidden Kingdom, the Wirral Peninsula, where we lived for some years.

effort, but otherwise anywhere. Being of a delicate disposition, i.e. a wimp, I decided to not choose following a contact sport of any sort. This also ruled out the martial arts, which I did consider seriously as the beautiful Japanese wife and I had friends involved in a variety of such oriental disciplines. Being a vegetarian ruled out any sport involving animals as my psychology of the relationship of humans to other organisms was already over sophisticated for most people's tastes, if not mine.

In the end I chose Test cricket, a game I knew nothing about. I'd batted once in my life, at school, out for a golden duck, a French cricket upsie easily caught, thank goodness, as there were no pads and the fast-ish bowler, I think he was called Gorse, was a year older than the rest of us, and big lad to boot. I remain indebted to my colleague in the Department of Computer Science at the University of Liverpool, Dr. Trevor Bench-Capon, for convincing me over a few beers that cricket was a truly complicated game, for the connoisseur, to be leisurely enjoyed unlike the eighty or ninety minute dash of rugby or football.

Cricket commentary was quite different around 1990 from today, where now I can stream, for free, live cricket on television and radio most days of the year. Back then it was Test Match Special on long wave and some occasional television, watched on a black and white portable. Trevor was right, cricket was very complicated, which delighted me because it clearly provided an intellectual challenge and, without this, I'd be unlikely to retain any enthusiasm for long. I knew so little that after my first couple of months I was at a garden party with Trevor and I remember him using a paper plate, a nearly clean one, to draw out the basic fielding positions; he started with, "You do know the difference between leg and off, don't you?" "Ummm, I think so, but put it on the plate."

My understanding of cricket, still howsoever humble, has improved since then, but the basic premise, that Test cricket is the most complicated game in the world, has stood the test of time. As I summarise to those who know not cricket, it's a psychological game, of individuals within a team context, where conditions change over five days. The ball changes its properties as it gets older and the wicket will deteriorate, and there's always the weather to contend with. You've got to understand it's language, and pay attention, because either the left or the right side of the field may be the off or leg side depending on whether the batsman is right or left handed. This is usually more than sufficient for the cricket know-nots and I can return to watching the cricket on my club's television (as a Northern city boy, I was horrified to discover in 1996 that I'd bought a house in Bournemouth in a pub-lite zone, hence "my club" as the nearest watering hole).

Since I retired as a full time academic in 2006, and as recently I've done less work as a consultant, I have been able to devote myself evermore to cricket. For Christmas 2012 I started my cricket book collection, buying second hand copies on the internet for 1p plus £2.80 post and package. I will have more than a hundred by the time this book is published, and I will have read all of them several times. I still enjoy modest royalties from my science and engineering publishing, so if I ever make any money from this book, then I promise I will make a donation to a cricket related charity to cover these cricket book authors' missed royalties.

An old slogan of mine is, 'I think, therefore I write'. I have enjoyed writing this book and doing so has had the additional advantage that the beautiful Japanese wife, we've been together more than three decades, not only lets me watch cricket on the radio (and occasionally on television) *all day*, but actively encourages me to do so, because I am "working". Envy me, I refer to her as the bJw for excellent reasons.

Chapter 2

Bowlers' Spurs.

In the famous game between England and Britannula [1], England won the toss and elected to bat, bringing the openers and baronets, Sir Kennington and Sir Lords, to the crease. It is reported of Sir Kennington that, "As he took his place upon the ground there was great cheering. Then the steam-bowler was ridden into its place by the attendant engineer". After around a quarter of an hour attending to and sighting the machine, "there came a sharp snap, a little smoke, and lo, Sir Kennington Oval was – out!"

I am looking forward to the updated, Hollywood, all-action movie. The steam catapult bowling machine might be called 'The Fiery Fred' and manufactured by Trueman's Ltd., 'The Bloody Fastest Steam Bowling Machines in the World'. How could such a technologically innovative future cricket have come about? I suspect that the MCC would have had to have been of a very different character in the 19th. and 20th. Centuries.

As a scientist I may only assume the existence of the 'real world', but my task is to understand it and I cannot change the universe to suit my theories and experiments. In contrast, the administrators can change the rules, or laws, of their sport as they wish, on a whim, or, it is possible, if rare, rationally. Cricketing authorities have a long history of stamping on technical innovation, although one can hardly fault Hambledon's making an "iron frame, of the statute width" [2] in 1771 once "Thomas 'Shock' White came to the crease with a bat as wide as the wickets" [3]. Apparently White's home-made bat had a knife taken to it by a Hambledon player before an angry

White was allowed to use it [4].

Of more questionable merit was the revision of Law 6 in 1980 that "the blade of the bat shall be made of wood". This change came about after Dennis Lillee arrived at the crease in the Perth Ashes Test of 1979 with an aluminium bat. After a few balls, England's captain, Mike Brearley, objected on the quite reasonable grounds that the bat was damaging the ball. After an unsightly kafuffle and much ill temper from Lillee, he was forced to abandon his metal bat which, it is reported, he and a backer had spent £0.4 Million developing [5].

Why must cricket bat blades be made only of wood? If golf had the same conservative attitude as MCC, then they'd still be playing with hickory shafted clubs. It is an easy, very lazy decision for a committee to simply ban all innovation in an area. Who knows, there may have been innovations in materials and composites that, overall, would have benefited cricket, but all research on these is forbidden by MCC's simplistic blanket ban. In support of such criticism, a more sophisticated revision of the Laws would have been to ban bats which significantly damaged the ball.

There have, of course, been innovations in bat design in recent decades, the willow becoming less pressed, changes in shape have been tried and, of late, bats with much thicker edges. There seems almost universal agreement amongst cricket commentators that it is easier to hit the ball further with modern bats. Whether this is a good thing for cricket, however, is moot. Had MCC taken a more sophisticated approach in 1980, then they, and later ICC, would subsequently have had to consider other aspects of bat design, whatever materials they were made of. Then, they would have been in an informed position to decide whether even the modern design of wooden bats were, overall, of benefit to cricket.

As a research engineer I am in love with design. I publish papers on what it is to do design, about the psychology of its creative aspects, and that, fundamentally, design is about predicting futures. I use the plural 'futures' here deliberately, for very complicated reasons, but successful design is one of the great intellectual challenges, because you can be wrong, demonstrably and expensively. So, I design cricket stuff, for the love of it.

Quite a few years ago I came up with the idea of bowlers' spurs. In their simplest form, like those of horse riders of yore, they would project from the heel of a bowler's boot and so would lessen the chance of bowling front foot no balls as the spur would be behind the line even when the bowler's boot encased foot was well over. How long could these heel extension be and still allow a fast bowler to run in? In my extreme Victorian design, the spur would be vertical, behind the bowlers calf, and hinged at the heel so that on the delivery stride, where the heel hits the ground hard, a catch is automatically released which, by springs, snaps the spur down to a horizontal position, the spur's tip touching the ground.

Such sprung loaded technology would quite rightly be banned, but the basis of the ban should be made with care. Whimsical may be my musings during slow periods of play, but I can see a practical, and legal, spin-off. Bowlers' boots, with modern materials and technology, might these days be better described as trainers. I'd design these with an extended ball shaped heel. The justification would be based on physiology, bio-mechanics and so forth, that the ball shaped heel allowed the bowler's ankle to rotate smoothly and so reduce impact stress and, therefore, injuries. All highly desirous, but really it's just a heel extension to give bowlers a few millimetres edge, which may not sound much, but front foot no balls have come under increasing scrutiny from third umpires using video so that even millimetres have become crucial.

Years before my first bowlers' spurs design, David (Bumble) Lloyd tells the tale of David Steele suffering a front foot no ball problem in the 1980s [6]. Reporting that Steele had size eight feet, he borrowed a size eleven boot, just the one, from a team mate. The denouement, if you can trust Bumble not to let the truth get in the way of a good story, was that starting his next bowling spell, Steele "delivered ... a no ball." That shows the real problem with developing bowlers' spurs or any other form of heel extension to help fast bowlers, they'll just take the extra and still bowl the same number of no balls. Sigh!

I love design and I've spent many happy hours tucked up in bed before I nod off designing cricket grounds with roofs that would cover the ground when it rained. The challenge is the size of cricket grounds. I've played with designs in the traditional materials of concrete, steel and glass, cantilevered, box girder and geodesic, and with modern light materials using wires, pneumatics or hydraulics.

What about the design of cricket balls? British Duke balls are hand made by craftsmen from natural materials. It is recognised that even from the same batch, some balls will perform differently from others. That bowlers believe that a "darker cherry" is better for swing bowling may be correct, or it could be just an empirically untested superstition. Even if superstition, psychologically it is not mere, as if a bowler believes a ball will swing well, then it is more likely to due to subtle changes in the bowler's action caused by the belief. It's easier to understand the converse, the bowler thinks, "This bloody pink thing will never swing.", so, unsurprisingly, it doesn't.

Is inter-ball variability a good thing for cricket? There must be a traditional view that it is, that it is all part of the rich tapestry that adds delicious complexity to the great game of cricket. I shall not contest, but if it is a good thing for cricket, then what is the optimal range of variation in a population of cricket balls? Are cricket balls, these days, too similar? Should we introduce more variation? To do so would be to deliberately introduce faults into the manufacturing process, to not produce the best, most consistent balls possible. Also, what would be the nature of these "faults"?

"It's a batsman's game.", is a common moan from

bowlers, which at times has had some justification. Many things have been tried to even up the balance of the competition between bat and ball, for example, having bigger stumps. Different ball designs have been tried. Simon Hughes [7, p220] tells of the Test and County Cricket Board in 1989 recommending the Reader ball "because it kept its shape better." Described, with litotes[2], as "well received" by bowlers,

> *"... the Reader had a huge, thick seam so proud you could cut your fingers on it. ... It zigged and zagged off any grassy surface, and the right-angled break-back, a delivery which had become extinct with the advent of lifeless, covered pitches, was reborn".*

It is a batsman's game and the following year they changed to a near seamless "orange" of a ball and so ushered in the Year of the Bat. Not to trivialise, Hughes points out that this decision "terminated several bowlers' careers".

Long I've pondered on the design of cricket balls. At my most extreme, I've considered inserting a metal slug within the ball to introduce an asymmetry in flight. The fun is then to work out where the weight would be placed within the ball and what effect different locations might have, for different types and speed of bowling. Idle design on a wet afternoon it may be, but would it be a more useful possibility than a bowler's steam catapult? I dedicate this chapter to cricket commentators everywhere who need to fill time in lunch, tea and rain intervals, who may now ask their colleagues, "Well, what do think of this proposal to slug balls?"

---

[2] Ironical understatement, said to be much the style of David Gower.

[1] Trollope, A. (1882) *The Fixed Period.* Reprinted in Haining, P. (1986) *LBW – Laughter Before Wicket: A Century of Humorous Cricket Short Stories.* Robson Books.

[2] Major, J. (2007) *More Than a Game: The Story of Cricket's Early Years.* HarperCollins.

[3] Birley, D. (1999) *A Social History of English Cricket.* Aurum.

[4] Scott, L. (2009) *Bats, Balls & Bails: The Essential Cricket Book.* Bantam.

[5] Benson, R. (2011) *The Cricket Lover's Companion.* Summersdale.

[6] Botham, I. (2013) *Beefy's Cricket Tales: My Favourite Stories from On and Off the Field.* Simon & Schuster.

[7] Hughes, S. (1997) *A Lot of Hard Yakka – Triumph and Torment: A County Cricketer's Life.* Headline.

Chapter 3

Better than a Hat Trick. What do you call it?

I was fortunate to be watching on the radio every ball of the third morning's play between Somerset and Sussex at Taunton on Tuesday, 10th. June, 2014. My early email to the commentators, Adrian Harms (BBC Radio Sussex) and Stephen Lamb (BBC Radio Bristol), had described the state of the match as "beautifully balanced" and I was looking forward to two more days of excellent cricket, and commentary, as the weather was set fair. What then happened was very exciting, but, alas, meant there was no fourth day of play for me to enjoy.

Somerset's seamer Alfonso Thomas entered the record books at the age of 37, taking four wickets in four balls; a feat last done in the English County Championship fourteen years before and which has only been done thirty seven times in all major forms of international cricket, according to 'ESPN Cricinfo'. So, it is a rare event.

As I recall, Thomas' first three deliveries of the over to Sussex's James Anyon were dots, "roughing up the batsman", according to the commentators. Then came the hat trick of Anyon, Rory Hamilton-Brown and the Sussex captain, Ed Joyce. Out in three different ways: bowled, lbw and caught behind, respectively. Peter Trego bowled the next over, a wicket maiden, taking the Sussex opener Chris Nash, on twelve, with the fourth ball. Alfonso then took his fourth wicket, that of Mathew Machan, with the first ball of the next over, thus taking four wickets in four balls.

To Adrian Harms credit, he let Stephen Lamb give the radio commentary of the hat trick ball. The excitement on the radio was great, both considerable and entertaining, particularly as on reflection, neither commentator had ever witnessed a first class hat trick before. Following Trego's wicket they had hardly the breath left to whisper that Thomas could get "four-in-four", which he duly did.

With an overnight score of 26-0, Sussex were reduced from 33-0 to 33-5 in ten balls. It took the rest of the day to bowl them out for 178 and for Somerset to win by six wickets, scoring 107 for 4 in 20.1 overs. As these figures suggest, it was a full day of exciting cricket.

The radio cricket commentary was even more exciting. While Adrian and Stephen admitted they still hadn't recovered before the lunch interval, they encouraged emails and tweets, indeed, they said they were, and wanted to be, "inundated". They called for 'The Statisticians' to dust off their record books, although why they think all such are Bill Frindall-like bearded was a lapse that privately amused me, "What, even all the female ones?"

Bearded or not bearded, as The Statisticians beavered away I snuck in with a quick stat of my own, part of which was read out on the radio as:

> 9 in 9 balls.
> Blenheim, New Zealand, December 1967:
> Marlborough College 'A' v. Bohally Intermediate School.
> Stephen Fleming (14) took nine wickets in nine balls.

I nicked this from Andrew Ward's 'Cricket's Strangest Matches' [1], found quickly by just skimming its Table of Contents. Then the more interesting and less facetious numbers started to come in via email and tweets.

Often I've mulled on cricket's rich, eclectic, redundant and incomplete terminology; why don't we have a word for the start of play, equivalent to 'stumps' at the close of a day?[3] Thus, I wondered, what might one call four wickets

---

[3] I have gleaned that there is a term from the following quote from an old letter to the Daily Telegraph, January, 1955: "why it is that wickets are pitched to start the day's play but stumps are

in four consecutive balls by the same bowler? Adrian Harms and Stephen Lamb could certainly have used a term equivalent to 'hat trick' as they had to stumble repeatedly over some version of "four wickets in four consecutive balls" for listeners arriving later in the morning, and throughout the rest of the day.

My next email to the commentators, written in the lunch interval, had the title "What should we call it? A Collective Opportunity/Competition." The email said:

> We've a rich cricket lexicon, so what should we call getting 4 wickets in 4 consecutive balls?
> All your e-mailers and tweeters have an opportunity to decide this afternoon, on BBC local radio, what we will call this "four-for-four".
> I look forward to your expert judicial decisions on who can suggest the best neologism (new-word).
> A good way to mark the occasion!
> All excellent, cricket and commentary.
> Dr. Dan <>

Read out not long after the resumption of play, this produced quite a good response from an international audience. Favoured by the commentators were a 'Range Rover' and an 'Audi'.

Probably against 'Range Rover' is the BBC's anti-advertising policy, of which I am thoroughly grateful, and commentators having to say something like, "... and other four-by-four Chelsea Tractors are available from a number of manufacturers." This rather defeats the aim, of brevity, for having a new term.

The same might also apply to an 'Audi', but the argument against this otherwise worthy proposal is that it would be better reserved for an even more remarkable

---

drawn to end it?" [2, pp4, 54-5]. My point is that in a quarter of a century, I've never heard a commentator use some variation of this meaning of 'pitch', for example, "The wickets are pitched and we are ready for the first ball of the day."

bowling feat: four wicket *ducks* in four consecutive balls by the same bowler. Then the scorecard really would have the Audi emblem of four noughts. Unfortunately for Alfonso Thomas, he didn't manage this as his first victim, Anyon, had opened and made eighteen before his dismissal. On the plus side for an 'Audi' is that if it ever happened, then five ducks in five consecutive balls could be call an 'Olympic'.

To credit the taste of all those who responded to my competition, I don't think anyone suggested things as vulgar as a "super hat trick". Furthermore, there is no agreement amongst cricket writers as to the origin of the term 'hat trick'. Proposals range from the obvious, that a collection was made in a hat, which may or may not have then been the stake for a wager on taking the third wicket, to a hat being awarded as a prize to the bowler. The latter is not as odd as a cricket history neophyte might suppose, given the many odd things used as prizes in the early days of cricket, for example, eleven pairs of gloves, and hats were expensive items then, and, until very recently, professional cricketers were, in any case, appallingly rewarded.

On such a historical basis, my own, admittedly modest, proposal for four wickets in four balls was a 'hat and suit trick'. In defence of this, achieving five wickets in five balls could then be a 'hat, suit and shoes trick' and we could add further items of apparel for ever more consecutive wickets. Thus the young Stephen Fleming mentioned previously as achieving nine wickets in nine consecutive balls might be described as bowling a 'hat, suit, shoes, shirt, gloves, waistcoat and gold watch chain trick.' It is perhaps fortunate for Master Fleming that he was removed from the attack after he had bowled only nine balls as ten out of ten, being too good to be true, might be marked by a more sinister reward, such as being investigated for throwing.

In conclusion, a marvellous day's cricket, and commentary, which the author was privileged to watch on the radio. Unfortunately, no decision was reached on what to call it when a bowler achieves four wickets in four consecutive balls. A shame as we may have a long time to wait to reignite this debate.

[1] Ward, A. *Cricket's Strangest Matches: Extraordinary but True Stories from 150 Years of Cricket.* Robson Books.

[2] Smith, M. (Ed.) (2011) *Not in My Day, Sir: Cricket Letters to The Daily Telegraph.* Aurum.

Chapter 4

Watching Cricket on the Radio.

> *"Cricket on the radio is a game of the imagination whereas cricket on television is a matter of fact."*
>
> Sandy Balfour [1]

For decades I'd tell people that I've been "watching cricket on the radio". Now too hackneyed for my own ears, the phrase still has the simple merits of: (a) being true; and (b) allowing me to test whether those new to this conversational gambit are paying attention.

If I do have my audience's attention, then I explain that the radio creates images in my mind, just as a book does; and we are used to combining auditory and visual inputs to create a composite, conscious percept – look what happens when a film's sound is out-of-synch with the pictures; and blind people do follow, and enjoy, cricket; and somewhere around here I've probably lost my audience.

Over a quarter of a century, most of the cricket I've seen has been on the radio. Judging from listeners' feedback over the years, many people have the radio on to listen to the cricket while they are doing something else. My watching cricket on the radio is rather more intense than this, perhaps akin to those who score a game for themselves. Basically, I focus all my attention on the cricket to the extent that I'm unable to do anything else, except, perhaps, reach for the conveniently located beverage.

Technically, attention involves 'the allocation of cognitive processing resources'. We are able to do more than one thing at a time (divided attention), but while the human mind is an incredibly powerful information processing device, ultimately even its resources are limited and so, when doing two mentally difficult tasks, either one, or both, will suffer performance deficits, taking longer, making more errors, or both. The extreme case is when language understanding is the primary task, as this requires nearly all of our mind's processing power so that secondary tasks suffer; it is for this reason that car driving, a very dangerous activity, should not be tried while using a mobile 'phone, even if it is 'hands-free'[4]. Over more than sixty years, there have been thousands of experiments published on attention, so the phenomena are well documented and are sufficiently robust that they are routinely part of undergraduate psychology degree experiments. To my professional chagrin, usefully applying this laboratory work to everyday life amongst the general population has been unsuccessful.

What I try to do when watching cricket on the radio is to follow each ball while keeping in mind all the fielding locations. It is the latter which is the mentally demanding task. I've found radio cricket commentators very good at relaying fielding positions and they all tend to use a similar shorthand for common patterns of field placements, for example, and said quite quickly, "two slips – gully – mid-on – mid-off – ...". Furthermore, a quirky position such as fly slip will usually be explicitly mentioned on the radio, as will happen when commentators disagree with a captain's field, very frequently, for example, that there is no third man.

Throughout a match I am trying to maintain this visualisation, but introspecting about it, it differs in many ways from television. First, I tend to have a circular mental map on which I place the fielding positions as,

---

[4] The point about mobile 'phones is that the other person does not have in-car context information, so, unlike a passenger, they will continue to try and have a conversation during a "tricky" bit of driving.

although cricket playing fields are rarely circular, it's hard to know their shape from most radio commentaries, although it is important to know about long or short boundaries, particularly in limited overs cricket.

Then, as the ball is bowled, I have a bowler's-list, left or right arm, over or round the wicket, pace or spin. The commentators will describe the batsman's stroke which I see in my mind's eye on a simple manikin. Then I follow the ball on my circular fielding map. The whole procedure is truncated for most dot balls and the key phrase, perhaps the most helpful general one in radio commentary, is "and there is no run". I give black marks to commentators who too often omit this key phrase as in their doing so I am often left not knowing whether a run was scored and thus the crucial information as to which batsman will face the next ball. In such circumstances I find myself listening as carefully as possible, playing the detective, which is additional effort I could really do without.

Before the advent of free ball-by-ball coverage on internet television, which covered most of my cricket watching life, I had two devices that I used to reduce the cognitive load, the amount of thinking effort my watching on the radio requires. These devices also reflect that I am not being provided with information that I am interested in as often as I want. First, I had a small, plastic but elegant, Japanese bowl on a small plastic tray and six marbles. I used these to record the balls in an over, not forgetting to remove a marble from the bowl in the event of a no ball. This device forces concentration as I'm miffed with myself if I discover at the end of the over that I've made a mistake.

My second device is a crib board. I use this to record the number of overs in an innings and from the start of a day's play. As I will know the score, information that the radio does provide with adequate frequency, then with my crib board I am able to do the basic mental arithmetic that lets me calculate the match's progress and consider options, tactics and, sometimes, strategies (Chapters 14 and 23). I try not to use a calculator because, like many people who are quite good at mathematics, I'm pretty poor at arithmetic. It goes back to my early school days and reports that mostly said, "needs to pay more attention." I'll also admit to being pretty poor at my alphabet as well. Internet television, or even just the scorecard from the BBC, means that, of late, my watching cricket on the radio devices gather dust on the window ledge.

I am sufficiently successful with my visualisations from radio that when, very occasionally, I later watch match highlights on my club's television, then usually I can accurately predict what happens to individual balls, such as, "The next one goes for four over extra cover." This isn't as hard as it sounds because the highlights still follow the real time sequence but with most dot balls omitted, and the scores at the bottom of the screen provide a major clue.

In recent years my summers have been filled with too many options of what cricket to watch. I have free access to nearly every international match, as virtually all are televised these days, and to the County Championship from BBC local radio from their website. Choosing which form of cricket to watch is easy, I prefer red over white ball and fifty over twenty overs. No gadfly, I strongly prefer to follow a single match but choosing which match to follow can be difficult, often between half a dozen County matches plus one or more internationals. Of all the criteria I balance in making my choice, almost the least important is whether a match is televised or not. It's not just stick-in-the-mud habit, overall I prefer watching cricket on the radio than on television, although I don't mind a combination of the two (Chapter 26).

Notwithstanding my preferences above, I will "watch", and can enjoy, any form of cricket. From my science and research engineering work, I'm used to spending days, weeks and, even, months concentrating on a single, complex set of problems to the exclusion of all else, save eating, drinking and sleeping. Thus, for me, a mere eight hours for five days of concentration is trivial.

My cricketing preferences, and how I watch cricket on the radio, are driven by my monomaniac approach to thought. Other people will have quite different personalities, knowledge and abilities, greater non-cricketing commitments and less generous opportunities to follow matches. Hence, other people, for good reasons, may have very different preferences. Cricket is a thinking person's sport, however, so my hope is that this chapter will stimulate thought in others, about why they follow cricket, what they enjoy, and encourage consideration of how, with some introspection, they might enjoy it even more.

[1] Balfour, S. (2009) *What I Love About Cricket.* Ebury Press.

Chapter 5

The Sound of Snicks.

For a couple of years either side of 1980, around ten of us lived rent free, with the University of Cambridge's Estate Department's blessing, in a Victorian mansion in one of the most expensive roads in Cambridge. Most of us were impecunious doctoral students and we called our house 'St. Kevin's College of Moral Theology and Metaphysics'. We held the ultimate May Ball most years, that's 'ultimate' meaning that it was always the last one of the season, but they were pretty good as well.

While at St. Kevin's, Dr. Peter Rich, a biochemist, and I played a game that we gleaned from a newspaper article. An African physicist, probably even more impecunious than us, was reported to have tested the urban myth that warm water freezes more quickly than cold water, and claimed that it wasn't a myth. Pete and I said, lets assume he's right, then how can we explain the phenomenon? To try to do so, we restricted ourselves to using no more than teenage school physics, or to be a bit more technical, to Newtonian Physics, which isn't all the work of Sir Isaac Newton, whatever the old so-and-so would have liked to claim.

We think we solved the water freezing problem and we then went on to create other problems that are everyday, but perplexing. For example, why do you have to put your foot on the ground when on a stationary bicycle? Or, why is it more tiring to walk upstairs then down?[5] I've kept up

---

[5] Gravity is NOT the answer. The problem is that one gains 'potential energy' ascending and one must lose *exactly* the same amount of energy descending. It's quite a lot of energy as can

this game since. As a way of thinking, it had serious applications in my theoretical research when I was Professor of Systems Science and Engineering. Stressing that I am not a physicist, now I want to apply it to the 'snickometer'.

I will also add a second caveat, that I do not intend to deal with the technology post-microphone, but will concentrate on the physics of ball striking bat. I assume that the electronic technology has been competently engineered, for example, that the frequency band pass filtering (the range of sound frequencies to which the system responds) of the microphone and any later processing is appropriate.

The idea behind the snickometer is very simple: if the ball hits the bat, then this will make a noise. Initially, the snickometer could not be used by the umpires because it took a couple of minutes to manually align the slow motion video and snickometer's audio feed. This is essential as there are other possible noises when the ball passes near the bat, such as striking another hard object such as a thigh pad or arm guard, or worse, the bat hitting the batsman's pads or, particularly, the toe of the bat striking the ground. As a technologist, I expected and so was unsurprised that by 2013 such video-audio alignment problems had been solved and the snickometer data could be used in a timely fashion as part of the Decision Review System (DRS).

These other potential noises illustrate the standard logical asymmetry that if A implies B, it does not follow that B implies A. So, if the ball hits the bat, then there will be a noise, but if there is a noise, it does not imply that the ball hit the bat, as the noise could be caused by other things in the few thousandths of a second when ball is near, but missing, the bat.

The technology works fine when ball and bat have a

---

be seen if it's all lost at once, on ground impact if you jump. Splat!

significant impact, otherwise we wouldn't bother with it. The issue, however, is how well the snickometer can detect extremely fine edges and the requirement, if it is to be useful, is that the snickometer is more sensitive, that it can better discriminate a hit from a miss, than just slow motion video alone, which relies on the third umpire having to make difficult decisions about whether there was a minute gap between ball and bat, or whether there was a slight deviation in the ball's flight or rotation caused by a fine impact. This leads to a fundamental question, 'What counts as a hit?'

To address this question, it is necessary to refer to the basic physics of energy transfer. At the level of teenage school physics, there are lots of different types of energy: kinetic, potential, heat, sound, and so forth. To understand the system one really needs an adequate model of physics at the next level down, a molecular model, which I use, but is beyond the scope of this chapter and any remaining enthusiasm of its readers.

The ball has a lot of kinetic energy because it a small, dense object moving quickly, so some of its energy is transferred to the bat. When the ball is struck cleanly down the wicket, then, on average, more energy may be transferred from bat to ball, the ball reversing its direction and leaving the bat faster than it arrived. With a very fine nick, however, average energy transfer will be to the bat, leaving the ball in a lower energy state, that is, travelling slightly more slowly.

Little sound will come from the ball, but when it hits, no matter how delicately, the bat is compressed, which sends shock waves through it's rigid structure, which acts as a sounding board. On the surface of the bat, the compression waves interact with air molecules which then mimic the vibration in the bat, thus causing a sound. A sound is simply the result of compression and rarefication of the air, but unlike tossing a pebble into a still pond and seeing a cross section in the ripples on the surface, in three dimensions sound waves are usually very complex, of many frequencies and amplitudes. Fortunately, the snickometer system ignores frequency information and on its oscilloscope display plots acoustic energy (from a window of frequencies) against time.

Now, the final bit of teenage physics. When the ball gets very close, but does not strike the bat, then the air between ball and bat is compressed which, of course, means that a sound is produced. This is shown on the snickometer's display as an egg shaped blob. The closer the ball to the bat the bigger will be this blob. At the molecular level there is not a point of contact but a zone of indeterminacy. Molecules are unimaginably tiny so, at the molecular level, compared to cricket's "corridor of uncertainty" (© G. Boycott, *ibid.*[6]) this zone of uncertainty is from the Earth to the Moon, if not even bigger.

Beyond the zone, there is sufficient energy transfer to the bat that a threshold is reached and a sharp spike is displayed by the snickometer, rising from the fat end of the blob that is caused by air compressed between ball and bat.

The snickometer can thus provide what is called in science and engineering an 'operational definition'. An operational definition is in contrast to a theoretical one and involves defining something by following a procedure. I do not understand why the operational definition concept is not part of the common parlance of those in the general population who purport to have an interest in science. Operational definitions abound. Even a simple thermometer is calibrated by an operational definition: at one atmosphere pressure, water's boiling point is used to fix one end of the temperature scale and that this may be assigned an arbitrary value, 212^0F or 100^0C (or even 0^0 in one early scale) reflects it's operational character, as opposed to Absolute zero, which is based on a theoretical definition.

The snickometer's operational definition is that the ball is deemed to have hit the bat if a spike appears that

---

[6] *Ibid.* – which just means 'all over the place'.

exceeds some criterion such as being half as high again as the blob on the display that represents non-contact air compression. If no spike appears, or one does but does not meet the criterion's threshold, then, *by definition*, the ball has missed the bat.

An alternative to the snickometer is 'hot spot'. The latter uses infrared imaging to detect the heat associated with the energy transfer that occurs when ball hits bat. The physics of both technologies is pretty similar, detecting a form of energy, acoustic or thermal, and both producing an operational definition of what constitutes ball hitting bat. In competition, neither technology is entirely superior to the other. This may reflect local environmental conditions, for example, the snickometer may be less sensitive when there is high background noise, from high winds if not from fans of the human persuasion; and hot spot may be less sensitive in hot conditions. Until a much better technology is produced, perhaps using active sensors (interferometry, anyone?), then what is done is to combine the two technologies' operational definitions with a logical OR. Thus, if either the snickometer or hot spot indicate that the ball hit bat, then it is deemed a hit, whatever the other technology indicates[7].

The physics really is very simple and discussion of snickometer displays does not warrant the time it receives in Test commentaries where the technology is predominantly used. What is missing, and I think should be corrected by ICC, is the explicit criterion that should be associated with the snickometer's operational definition. I've suggested that this should be that the contact spike exceeds some proportion of the noise associated with the ball closely approaching the bat. The third umpire could just use a ruler to measure this! On the other hand, it

[7] Note, it is worth here making the logic clear because, for example, if we were less trustful of the technologies, then we might use a logical AND and only deem that bat had hit ball if both technologies confirmed this.

probably wouldn't take many lines of program code for a computer to make this measurement and so leave the third umpire with a red or green light and not to have the bother of interpreting an energy by time oscilloscope display.

Do we want the machines to take over umpiring decisions? As a technologist, I think, 'Yes', but I do appreciate what may even be a majority opinion, that decreasing the random factors is not in the best interests of cricket. One of the major changes that reduced such randomness was the introduction of covered wickets, still much lamented by some, especially Geoffrey Boycott (even more *ibid.*). I'd certainly want to keep wickets different, in different parts of the world, and in England, although I'd be happy for low, slow ones that don't take spin to be rarer. To encourage further thought, an issue is whether potential umpire error is like the differences between wickets. I think they induce quite different types of randomness into matches. I'd prefer to minimise the former, umpires' errors, using the best technology possible, but keep the latter, the differences between wickets.

Chapter 6

The Radio Cricket Commentators' Crime.

My topic warrants a whole chapter to itself because it complains of the single, most annoying, by a long way, failure of every ball-by-ball cricket commentary on radio. "Is the batsman right or left handed?" Why will they not tell me? I cannot properly watch cricket on the radio without this vital information.

I've already tried to describe how I watch cricket on the radio (Chapter 4). I am visualising, holding in my mind, a model of the cricket field, where are the fielders, the bowler's approach and delivery, and to where the batsman strikes the ball, if he hits it. What I'm told on the radio is whether the ball has gone to off or to on/leg, and, hopefully, a bit more detail about where in the off or on/leg side the ball has gone. My visualisation is completely different, however, depending on the handedness of the batsman, which, to state the extremely obvious, determines whether the off side is to the left or right of the bowler. Why won't they tell me?

I have sent emails about this to various BBC local radio cricket commentators. I noticed that these had less chance of being read out than my emails on other topics. I even tried to embed my requests to keep telling me whether the batsman is right or left handed with other topics, but, more than once, this bit didn't get read out. When I have been successful with these emails, uniformly the success has been extremely limited. I'm immediately told the handedness of both batsman and, then, back to the usual. Sigh. I ask them to "please keep reminding me of the batsmen's handedness." What's so difficult with understanding 'keep' or other synonyms such as repeat, often, frequently, etc.?[8]

One of the main reasons I bother to stream live cricket as video is so that I can glance at the screen to check batsman handedness. Sometimes the lag between radio and video streams is excessive, in minutes, but I keep the video on just to remind myself about each batsman, and for the score, if I've not the scorecard in another window.

Some years ago with only the radio to follow The Ashes all night, I was reduced to listing the two squads and writing down 'L' or 'R' by each name during the first match. I updated this sheet as the squads introduced new players in subsequent Tests. I should not have to do this. I should be told, regularly, whether the batsman facing the next ball is left or right handed. At a minimum they could tell me when they relay the field placements.

I have a very simple solution, which will work even if all a listener has is a radio, and which comes at no cost to commentators:

- When describing the field placements, start by saying, "*To the Right/Left handed [name optional]* there's two slips, gully, mid-off, mid-on, ..." – or however the field is set.

As I've remarked elsewhere (Chapter 4), I've found all the radio commentators I've listened to be very good at describing fielding positions, which they reduce to a slick, quickly read out list in a fairly standard order (such as slips, gully, other short fielders, deep fielders). All I'm asking is that they start this list with a minimum of four additional words, one of which is either 'right' or 'left'. Nor am I

---

[8] I made a moral decision not to pester Martin Emmerson of BBC Radio Newcastle on this when I realised that he did read out everyone's emails and, while on batsman's handedness he is no better than everyone else, I felt he should not feel singled out for criticism about reporting handedness just because he is so good with emails and tweets (see Chapter 15).

asking the radio commentators to acquire new information as they must know whether the facing batsman is right or left handed to be able to place fielders on the off or on/leg side. As they oft say on the BBC's motoring TV programme 'Top Gear', "How hard can it be?"

I am aware that there is a big difference between what nicely trickles out of the radio and the complexity, and clearly chaos sometimes, within the commentary box. The swan metaphor is hardly extreme enough: the swan all serene above water while furiously thrashing around below the surface. I've heard more than one commentator say that they are forever multitasking, dealing with paper data, computers, mobile phones and, and I marvel at this, parallel audio feeds from other studios, for example, to provide regular updates to other BBC local radio stations. They do a great job, which is why I commend my solution above, because it really won't add to their multitasking burdens, if only they can learn and remember to start the fielding placements list with "*To the right/left handed ...*".

I'm very careful about using absolutes, boorishly treating them as logical ALL, but I have never, not once in over a quarter of a century, at least that I can recall, ever heard a radio commentator remind me with adequate frequency whether the currently facing batsman is right or left handed. This is strange.

My hypothesis is that cricket commentators have acquired an expert cognitive skill that, with much practice, they are unaware of using. Basically, they look at a cricket field and they automatically classify which is the off and on/leg sides. They are unaware of how they do this, but probably they use the general fielding positions more than they need to look at the facing batsman. Technically this would be an example of 'deep compiled knowledge' and the classic examples are bicycle riding and driving a car, although my introspections lead me to suggest that we have a great deal of this type of knowledge which we use very frequently. My own favoured example is how one moves around a home one has lived in for years, opening doors, switching on lights, confident even in the dark, with no apparent conscious effort.

A characteristic of deep compiled knowledge is that we use it to do, but cannot describe how we do what we do. The term widely and erroneously used in cricket circles is 'instinctive', which is the wrong word because, properly, instincts are genetically programmed behaviours and so different from skills that are acquired through learning[9]. As a species we haven't evolved much for quite a long time, so claims for anything merely historical being in one's DNA is utter nonsense; I shudder.

My hypothesis is that radio cricket commentators share a universal mental blind spot. They so automatically, without conscious effort, classify the field that they have difficulty understanding that just telling their listeners off or on/leg side is actually meaningless without the critical information on the facing batsman's handedness. Typically, deep compiled knowledge is not like a computer program, but is used flexibly and appropriately in a variety of situations. Better than the software analogy, such knowledge is a mental adjustable spanner which can be used to tighten or loosen a wide range of nuts and bolts in a wide range of different situations, but is still of limited functionality, so it doesn't make a very good mental hammer or screwdriver.

Deep compiled knowledge is not only learned, but learning usually continues, which is why car drivers do get better after their first few tens of thousands of miles, and partly why their insurance premiums get better over some decades of driving. Therefore, now it has been pointed out to them, radio cricket commentators should be able to

---

[9] Or, perhaps better and probably more frequently and importantly, instincts are genetically programmed predispositions for the brain to become organised in particular ways, provided appropriate stimulation is offered to the organism. To those readers who can accept vivisection, at least at second hand, then look up the work of Prof. Colin Blakemore on cortical plasticity in kittens.

slightly modify their deep compiled, mental script and to always start reporting the field setting with the words, "*To the right/left handed ...*".

Belt and braces, I have also suggested that batsmen's handedness could easily be added to the team lists as displayed on the BBC website's scorecards (Chapter 20). My "*To the right/left handed ...*" solution, however, will work for everyone listening, even those who have only a radio. Thinking of everyone, apart from meeting my own needs, anyone who has just tuned in to a radio cricket commentary has the same problem that I have and while one never has long to wait for the score, who is batting and bowling, or how the field is set, then, unless a wicket falls, it can be tens of minutes before the batsmen's handedness is mentioned. For all this time no new listener can know which side is the off side and which the on!

I'll admit that, unless I write it down, I do forget the batsmen's handedness, even during a session, particularly if I'm unfortunately interrupted, even briefly. It is certainly beyond me, in terms of time and effort, to memorise team lists and handedness. The numbers are large. In a year I'd need to memorise, for say a squad of 15, 18 County teams and 9 Test sides, which is over 400 players[10].

While it might be taxing to explain to a cricket neophyte, the rotation of the off and on/leg sides depending on whether the facing batsman is right or left handed is quite sensible and, also, isn't some ancient design fault. It's a sensible convention because it maintains the standard fielding locations to the off and on/leg sides as it is assumed that left handed batsmen play similar shots to right handed ones, but to the opposite side. Human physiology determines, excepting drives down the ground, that off side shots are different from on/leg ones, hence standard fielding positions differ between the off and on/leg sides.

I say there isn't a design fault with the convention on

---

[10] (18 x 15) + (9 x 15) = 27 x 15 = 405

the grounds that it is very hard to design a better replacement. Answers on a postcard, or email, please, but using the view from the bowler's end has its own problems. For example, replacing "hits it to mid on" with "hits it to mid right" are still only the same shot if the batsman is right handed. What would one replace specialist positions such as third man with? I know it is on the off side, but from the bowler's perspective it would be something like "left fine deep" for a right handed batsman and "right fine deep" to a left handed batsman, which leaves one right fine deep in it.

Historical inertia is against any change in the naming convention of mirroring the field placements of right handed batsmen for left handed ones. It is not without merit. My simple, virtually cost free in every way, solution is for all radio cricket commentators, when they are going to tell their listeners how the field is set, to start with "*To the right/left handed ...*".

Please. Practice, "*To the right handed ...*", "*To the left handed ...*", "*To the right handed ...*". It would make me very happy. Thank you. Pleas and Please.

Chapter 7

Trophies and Tribulations.

'Trophies and Tribulations: Forty Years of Kent Cricket' [1] is a heavy book. My second hand hardback, signed by the authors, has those shiny pages which, even if it's modern technology, feel like they are glazed in old fashioned china clay, which is, after all, stone. It weighs 1lb.10oz., or three quarters of a kilo to metric familiar readers.

Ergonomics is the engineering discipline of matching designed objects to the human body, such as making seats to fit the shape of people's bums. Cognitive Ergonomics matches things to the shape of people's minds. So why design a book which is difficult to hold and difficult to read because the pages are heavy and reflective. I often had to tip the book to read the edge of the page near the book's spine. Furthermore, this book will probably have a more mature readership, including myself, so good design by the publishers is even more important.

This is a heavy book. Who can love this book who know not love of Kent? I enjoyed it more on my second reading. On both readings, I enjoyed more Part III by Mark Pennell, than Clive Ellis' first two parts, but the authors' styles are not inconsistent. Both authors spent years reporting Kent matches for the local newspaper, the Kent Messenger. They thus have the twin advantages of long term expertise on their topic and a little distance from, but access to, the dressing room and Kent's management.

The book is arranged chronologically. After an historical introduction by Ellis, covering 1711 to 1966, his Part I, "Glory Days", covers 1967 to 1978 and his part II, "Wilderness Years", 1979 to 1992. Part III, "False

Dawns" by Pennell in chapters six to ten covers the years 1993 to 2009. This is a lot of cricket to condense into 288 pages. I think it unfair criticism to say that, in places, reading is heavy going without taking into consideration that the authors manage to provide so much detail over four decades of matches. Given the authors' professional writing background, the book is very well written and could stand as a model of its genre. Unless one is a loyal Kent fan, however, it is only likely to appeal to the mature cricket connoisseur. I enjoyed the book, but I'm not sure I can fully recommend it to a wider readership.

Also, I value this book. It has provided me with an excellent example that I use in another chapter (Chapter 8) and one of my favourite cricket quotes of the thousands that I've collected: "The main thing is cricket's a great game – it's just played by idiots." (p215). So said former Australian captain Bobby Simpson in 1999 while coaching at Kent.

Such a useful quote, and too good to be wasted just to put Ellis' view into context that when the Gillette Cup was introduced in 1963, "Kent, in common with most of the other sides, were slow to grasp the tactical demands of the original 65-overs competition." (p24). I think similar comments could be made of many rule changes and more recently of Twenty20 cricket. For example, I've enjoyed the tactical improvements that I've seen over the first seven years of the Indian Premier League. Perhaps the international teams really do need an army of analysts, specialists who are not ex-players, if it is a game played by idiots, flannelled fools, indeed.

[1] Ellis, C. and Pennell, M. (2010) *Trophies and Tribulations: Forty Years of Kent Cricket.* Greenwich Publishing, U.K.

Chapter 8

What's the Difference? It's All in the Mind.

For once living up to it's moniker, 'Flaming June', (historically it is one of the wettest months of the year in England), Wednesday the 11th., 2014 was a "nice day" for playing cricket. Unfortunately, the Yorkshire versus Nottinghamshire County Championship match had been previously rain affected and the afternoon's play was "petering out" to "an inevitable draw", which the captains eventually agreed to at around five o'clock.

Such circumstances are hard times for live cricket commentators. Fortunately, on BBC local radio there were those doyens of discussion, the three Dave's, Callaghan, Bracegirdle and, guesting, Townsend. There is only so much humour to be extracted by Cally and DT referring to the other Dave as 'The Girdler' or similar. DT produced one of his perfectly crafted gems of a grump at a disintegrating mobile 'phone, supposing it was bought from a market stall for a fiver and probably made in China. Then their idle banter turned to a cricket question: *What is the difference between a rank long hop and a slow ball bouncer?*

Physically, the Daves agreed, there was no difference. Meandering around the question, they eventually came up with the notion that the difference was psychological, that it involved the bowler's intent. Thus, a long hop is a mistake whereas the slow ball bouncer is deliberately bowled.

So, what might a scientific psychologist make of the three D's notion? A fairly obvious start can be made by breaking it into two components: (a) physical; and (b) psychological. This leads to the questions: (A) Are the two types of ball bowled identical?; and (B) Is it reasonable to distinguish them on the assumed psychology of the bowler? As is so often the case with biologically orientated research science and engineering, the critical concept involves categorisation.

From the experimental psychologists' laboratories we know, even for very simple tasks, that human behaviour is never identically repeated. At the other extreme, all that is being claimed is that commentators cannot visually tell the difference between a rank long hop and a slow ball bouncer at their viewing distance. These are just two of the many classes of balls that might be bowled and each of these types will have a number of properties which either must or could be fulfilled. These properties can be discrete and may be mutually exclusive, for example either pitching on leg or on off, but never both. Alternatively, the properties that distinguish classes of ball may be parameters, such as the speed at which the ball leaves a bowler's hand, as estimated by a commentator or measured by radar. Such parameters when, in part, are used to categorise types of ball bowled may overlap, say for a medium-fast bowler and a fast-medium one. The point here is that classifying balls bowled into types, based on physical properties, often is far from straightforward.

Turning to question (B) concerning classifying balls bowled by the bowler's psychology, I can see no problem, in principle, with this, but do point out that if the psychology is sound, then there would be physical differences that could be detectable under laboratory conditions.

A critical word in question (B), however, is 'assumed', that is, that the commentator has to assume that they understand, in some sensible and reliable way, the psychology of the bowler. Really? Would anyone really want to 'get into the mind of a bowler', or, more accurately perhaps, understand what the bowler believes is in their mind when they bowl a ball? I'm afraid this is rather typical, but good and necessary, double-think for psychologists. Thus, we have the possibility of a commentator's model of a bowler's psychology, or, a commentator's model of a bowler's model of their psychology. Unless you are a professional psychologist, then such thinking, at best I think, is mentally unhygienic. Naturally, commentator error is likely, will probably be frequent and certainly inevitable at times.

To illustrate such error, Ellis and Pennell [1, pp180-182], reporting on the Lancashire v. Kent, 1995 Benson and Hedges cup final at Lord's, note, and include a photograph, that while batting David Fulton wore a "wide-brimmed sun hat on his cup debut". They say that Fulton subsequently insisted that the hat was "down to insecurity rather than vanity. It wasn't a 'look-at-me moment', although a lot of people probably thought that was the case. The reality was that I was really nervous." To add to this further, Fulton's quote ends with the following: "I've seen recordings of the game since and it looks like I'm chewing gum, but I didn't have any gum with me; it was just nerves."

A cup final debutante's nervous disposition isn't very complicated psychology, and might be sufficiently simple that even a professional cricket player might be trusted to be able to describe their own mental state. The contrast is that others, commentators in whatever media, might suggest that wearing the sun hat was vanity thus illustrates the difference between the commentators' models of the player's mind and that of the player's model of their own mind.

Kent lost, their fifth consecutive loss in the final. David Fulton was out for 25, leg before wicket. His careful planning about nervousness reducing headgear, days before the match, can't be described as an unbridled success. A good psychologist, of whatever sort, will always use skilled observation of their subject's behaviour, including their physical behaviour, what they do, and their verbal behaviour, what they say and how they say it. If one can't tell if someone's chewing gum or not, then this necessary, careful observation doesn't appear to be available at the commentators' viewing distance.

From the above it might be tempting to conclude that it is not a realistic proposition for commentators to classify types of ball bowled based on the assumed psychology of the bowler, for example, whether they intended what they bowled. This conclusion, however, may still be in error.

What is missing from the above, and what is fundamental, is context. My impression is that the slow ball bouncer was primarily a 21st. Century development associated with the shorter forms of the game and most often used, deliberately, in the final, 'at-the-death' overs. Rank long hops have been with us for ages. Commentators may thus be on much safer grounds distinguishing these two types of ball by the context within the match and, also, historical context.

Match context is easier in the limited overs games because power plays with their fielding restrictions add additional structure which is often far less clear with red ball cricket, which for days may be open-ended as one can't know for how long a team will bat. Historical context might include knowledge that a bowler regularly bowls slow ball bouncers in appropriate match contexts, such as towards the end of white ball games. Similarly, it's a rank long hop when a seamer bowls this to the wrong side of a seven-two field on the first day of a Test match.

In conclusion, if commentators wish to distinguish between a rank long hop and a slow ball bouncer and they cannot see any physical differences, then they are on much safer grounds using the match and historical contexts as opposed to trying to guess what is in the mind of a bowler, or what a bowler thinks is in his mind. Using context is generally what they currently do and, after all, a great deal of live cricket commentary is about the context of the current match and its broader contexts within competitions and in comparison to other matches. Using such context, commentators won't always be right about such differences in balls bowled, but I'd prefer them not to claim a dubious psychological understanding, leaping in where the professionals are cautious to tread, although I do thank the three Dave's for enlivening a slow period of play on the final day at Headingley.

[1] Ellis, C. and Pennell, M. (2010) *Trophies and Tribulations: Forty years of Kent Cricket.* Greenwich Publishing, U.K.

Chapter 9

Better than a Hat Trick? A Double.

The psychoanalyst Carl Jung developed his concept of synchronicity to explain how events may be related by meaning as opposed to being related in the physical world of cause and effect. Ten days after Somerset's Alfonso Thomas took four Sussex wickets in four balls (Chapter 3), on 20th. June, 2014, England's Stuart Broad took a hat trick of Sri Lankan wickets. Also like the match a few days earlier, a wicket for no runs was taken, Dhammika Prasad's by Liam Plunkett, in the over that intervened within Broad's hat trick. Sri Lanka lost four wickets in nine balls for one run.

For the record books, Stuart Broad became the first England player to have ever taken two hat tricks in Test matches; his first was against India in 2011. Only three other players have taken two Test hat tricks: Pakistan's Wasim Akram, also against Sri Lanka, both in 1999; Australia's Hugh Trumble against England in 1902 and 1904; and, still uniquely, Australia's Jimmy Mathews who, against South Africa in 1912, took two hat tricks in the same match!

Broad took his wickets on the sixth ball of one over and the first and second of his next. There was a hilarious triumph for the BBC's Test Match Special when Vic Marks correctly spotted the hat trick, which went completely unnoticed by everyone else at Headingley, players, spectators and the television team, who on-screen still printed, incorrectly, that Broad was "on a hat trick". It was a couple of minutes before everyone caught up with TMS. England's captain, Alistair Cook, even maintained an aggressive field, lots of slips, for what he still thought was Broad's hat trick ball, whereas the hat trick had already been achieved with the wicket in his previous over. Notwithstanding this field placement, Broad didn't achieve taking four wickets in four consecutive balls.

As the TMS commentary crew ambled through various statistics about bowling records, it was pointed out that Broad had failed to take "four-in-four" and that in Australia this was called a 'double hat trick'. Here was my example of Jungian synchronicity. There is no causal relationship between the match at Taunton ten days before and the England v. Sri Lanka Test match. The two, however, were instantly related in my mind as I had enjoyed and been writing about the earlier match and I had instigated discussion on BBC local radio as to what we might call a four-in-four.

The rationale for the Australian double hat trick terminology is that the bowler has one hat trick with balls one, two and three, and then a second hat trick with balls two, three and four; balls two and three contributing to both of the hat tricks. The Australian logic is sound and if anyone does ever take five wickets in five balls[11], then this would simply be a 'triple hat trick', and so on for six balls, a quadruple hat trick, etcetera. Furthermore, the Australian terminology is quintessentially traditional cricket, beautifully obscure except to the cricketing cognoscenti. One just has to know that a double hat trick is four wickets in four consecutive balls and not, as the uninitiated might assume, a pair of separate hat tricks, as Broad has taken in his Test career.

Finally, to celebrate Test Match Special's mastery over commercial television, the radio commentary also pointed out that Stuart Broad is the only person to be involved in three Test match hat tricks. Unfortunately, in his third he was a batting victim to an Australian hat trick. Still, he is

---

[11] In 1964, Gary Sobers did take five wickets in five consecutive balls [1, p106] when playing for E.W. Swanton's Commonwealth XI against Malaysia in Kuala Lumpur.

the first England player, ever, to have two Test hat tricks, but not, sadly, a double one.

[1] Smith, M. (Ed.) (2011) *Not in My Day, Sir: Cricket Letters to The Daily Telegraph.* Aurum.

Chapter 10

Good Cricket?

A polysemous word is one that has more than one meaning. Is there a grammatical term for a polysemous word which has two distinct but opposite meanings? It would be a single word that was its own antonym. Until a linguist corrects me, I suggest that an appropriate neologism (new word) for this would be an ironym, as when people of my daughter's generation ironically once used 'wicked' to mean 'good'.[12]

The word I want to apply my ironym neologism to is 'fan'. In one sense a fan is a cooling device that moves air. Another meaning for fan is as an abbreviation of fanatic, and sports fans, metaphorically, create a great deal of hot, rather than cool, air. The latter type of fans have many other undesirable traits, such as loyalty, meaning blind, deaf and dumb (in the unintelligent sense) support whatever the contrary evidence. If only they were dumb in the auditory sense.

I've followed England Test cricket for about a quarter of a century; I was a late developer. The critical word in that sentence is 'followed'. I have never been a fan. What following England's (mis)fortunes has taught me is stoicism. My ancient 'Dictionary of Philosophy' [2], bought when I once taught such stuff, attributes stoicism to Zeno of Citium around 305 B.C. in Athens. The Stoics were influential for over half a millennium and proposed that the universe was rational and that everyone had their

---

[12] I am corrected by Bill Bryson [1, p63], the term I should use is a contranym, but my linguistic horse's *bolted* before the barn door's *bolted.*

ordained place in it, which they should jolly well accept. Just as the poor professionals for most of cricket's history were forced to accept, if not believe, the social and moral superiority of the amateurs. This is all pretty nasty to a modern person, and even more so when the universe of interest is cricket, which I've never heard described as rational, even by it's greatest proponents, be they Victorian muscular Christians, Time Lords Hawke and Harris, or the hypocrite Pelham Warner who's bodyline words and the deeds were mismatched (see [3]).

I will believe that the MCC has finally improved when, or if, there is redevelopment at Lord's and the Warner stand is named after someone more worthy. I'd say the same for the Allen stand, although Gubby did defy Jardine in the 1931-2 bodyline series, but my politest description of his decades of later influence at MCC would be 'the dead hand of'.

Ignoring stoicism's nonsense about rationality and predestination (e.g. England don't *always* lose the Ashes), the relevant stoic concept for the England Test follower is apatheia:

> ***Apatheia*** is the psychological state of insensitivity or indifference to pleasures and pains, emotions, joys and grief, anxieties and mental elation. *Apatheia* is a state of tranquility of mind and body – a psychic detachment from mental and physical disturbances. [2]

If the cost is not sharing in the general public's ridiculously over-the-top celebrations when England do win The Ashes, bringing London to a standstill, awarding O.B.E.s, and meeting politicians, who, I think, should not be encouraged, then that is a price I will willingly pay for all the times England don't win the little urn. With apatheia, following cricket is an intellectual exercise, which can be enjoyed without the rampant emotional highs and lows of fans.

How did I develop this apatheia of which I am so fond?

The answer is a surprisingly simple one, what I want is 'Good Cricket'. Unfortunately, but not unsurprisingly, what constitutes Good Cricket turns out to be far from simple.

I'll confess to having been intellectually lazy over the decades when saying things such as, "I don't mind what the result is, provided it is good cricket." Without analysis, such statements really mean little, particularly when it involves the team you follow. Of course I'd prefer England to beat Australia, (Doesn't everyone who isn't Australian?[13]), and any other national side England play, but clearly any one-sided game can't be Good Cricket. I believe this to be true in all the major forms of cricket.

So, my first criterion for Good Cricket is a negative one, abjuring matches or series where one team completely dominates the other, whether they be 5-0 whitewashes or blackwashes. This seems safe enough, but what other criteria might there be? To try and establish some of these, I'm going to restrict myself below to the longer forms of the game, but my conclusions, I anticipate, can also be applied to the limited overs versions of cricket.

If the scores are close at the end of play, does this mean that it has been Good Cricket? The closest scores in cricket matches occur when any of four results are still possible sometime after lunch on the final day of play; the four possible results being: team A wins (and B loses); team B wins (and A loses); a draw; or a tie. Ties are rare, but there have been exciting finales when a team just manages to win a draw: Anderson and Panasar's last forty minutes Ashes stand for England at Cardiff in 2009 does "live long in the memory", in Anderson's [4, pp179-184]

---

[13] Some years ago I was watching on the radio an Ashes series and there was a phone link to New Zealand to one of their famous ex-players. The question from TMS was, being geographically close to Australia, did most Kiwis support England or Australia? The reply was that if England won, they would be insufferable, but the Australians were insufferable all the time.

and mine, for me because it was done by the tenth and eleventh batsmen.

It would be convenient if another criterion for Good Cricket were that all four results were possible late in a match because then one could identify instances of it by examining the record books. I leave such exercises to cricket's Statisticians. My suspicion, however, is that many, if not the majority, of matches where all four results are possible would, by comparing the records with extensive match reports, turn out to be judged Good Cricket. If so, then this is a good criterion to add to the list, i.e. my second, but there is a problem with it in that it can be applied to only a small proportion of cricket matches.

For most cricket matches, during the latter part of the final day there are usually two possible outcomes: a win for one side or a draw. Note, that 'most' here includes the many matches where nearly everyone, and this *must* include both captains, agrees that, saving a miracle, the outcome will be a draw. Consequently, a third candidate criterion for Good Cricket would involve matches where a win or draw on the final day are approximately equiprobable, nearly equally likely in plainer speak. Again, this could be checked against records and match reports.

The second and third criteria attempt to determine whether a whole cricket match was good cricket based on the situation in the final sessions of play on the last day. In science and engineering terms, they provide a metric so that a complex thing, here a whole match, can be measured and judged by something simpler, here the situation near the end of a match. It's similar to measuring temperature to represent more complex things such heat and the speed of molecules.

These criteria are heuristic rather than logical, the former being a rule of thumb whereas the latter, at least in the simpler logics, are all-or-none. As a heuristic, criterion 3 is not logically disproved, it is NOT FALSE, just because one can find an exception to the rule; and please spare me from any idiocy that 'the exception proves the rule', this is nonsense. My exception to criterion 3 was what inspired this chapter, a match which was not good cricket even though the final session was very close to a win for only one side, or a draw.

The match was the first Test between England and Sri Lanka at Lord's in June, 2014. England almost did, but couldn't after a Sri Lankan appeal to the third umpire, finally take the last wicket at the end of the final session. This was very exciting, but most of the rest of the match was pretty dull, as was generally agreed on TMS, on a wicket that was slow even by Lord's standards. I was sorely tempted to start following a County Championship match by the start of day three, even though that would only be on the radio, whereas I could stream both live video and Test Match Special to my television for the Test match. I like to finish what I start, so I did stick with the Test match, but an exciting final session was no recompense for the rest of the match.

Enjoying my apatheia, mere short bursts of excitement is over rated, particularly in a four or five day game. I can enjoy "slow passages of play", where no wickets fall and runs are scarce, if there is a good balance between bat and ball. This leads me to the positive, inverse of my first criterion, that a match is good cricket when the game seesaws over the days of a match, first one side, then the other, having the upper hand.

To conclude and summarise, this chapter's title would be more accurate had I appended 'Matches' to my 'Good Cricket' as I have not addressed what might be good cricket during some part of a match. One would be a stern critic to find matches that did not contain any good cricket. My three criteria, so far, for Good Cricket Matches are:

1. The teams' advantage alternates throughout the match and one team does not just dominate the other;
2. Towards the end of the match, all four results are

still possible;
3. Towards the end of the match, one team is close to a win while the other fights for a draw.

The second and third criteria are heuristic metrics that use data from the final session or two of a match to judge whether the match, as a whole, was a good one.

These criteria are not exhaustive. Indeed, they are just a start that I intend to develop further. The point, however, is that just saying one wants "Good Cricket" doesn't mean very much until one analyses what one means by the term. Other people will, no doubt, propose different criteria to mine based on their own needs, style, and personality, but they will have to think about it, which, to my mind, can only be a Good Thing.

[1] Bryson, B. (1990) *Mother Tongue: The Story of the English Language.* Penguin.

[2] Angeles, P.A. (1981) *A Dictionary of Philosophy.* Harper & Row.

[3] Frith, D. (2002) *Bodyline Autopsy.* Aurum.

[4] Anderson, J. (2012) *Jimmy: My Story.* Simon and Schuster.

Chapter 11

A Favourite Funny Funny Cricket Book.

There are many cricket books which are intended to be funny in the humorous sense. A subset of these are also funny, in the sense of strange or odd, in their format. These tend to be small books and may use idiosyncratic typography, layout and non-standard paper. Tyers and Beach's 'W.G. Grace Ate My Pedalo' [1] is a small book, but does have 150 crammed pages in a small font. The overall printing deliberately resembles that of pre-computer hot metal technology. There is clever, humorous artwork on most pages that have a suitable Victorian feel to them.

This is one of the successful small, humorous cricket books. I have enjoyed reading it several times and, after a while, I've happily dipped back into it again. This book would be an excellent present, provided one picked someone for whom it is suitable. First, it's not suitable for the visually handicapped.

The next criterion of readership suitability is that one has to be a serious cricket follower. If you've never heard of Freddie and his pedalo in the Caribbean, then certainly this book is not for you. Having heard of C.B. Fry would also help. Given a publication date of 2010, most of the cricketing references are in the 'noughties', but, as memories fade, I recommend purchasing this book sooner rather than later, if at all, as I suspect many of the jokes are time limited as the cricketing world rotates on.

The final criterion may be hardest to fill, the reader needs a good sense of humour and, for sure, more than the egocentric, inevitably promised GSOH (Gosh!) of dating services. One might charitably describe the jokes as schoolboy or juvenile, if not childish, but what clever children! I found it like watching a television comedy programme from the 1970s and, if in modern, now accepted implicitly, political correctness mode, then one can cringe at the jokes, many of which are racist, sexist, classist, but, oddly, not anti-vegetarianist. Ignore such and let the light froth rinse you in puerile humour. Of course it has anti-Australian jokes, but given their history, and defence, of sledging ("mental disintegration" for goodness sake), then they reap what they for decades have sown.

The central conceit is the inheritance of the lost, first four issues of 'The Wisden Cricketer' of 1896. The book purports to be a miniaturised facsimile of these recently discovered magazines.

Occasionally the book faces the problem of parody, which is that to be funny, the parody needs to be more extreme than its target. Consider the following three quotes from readers' letters:

> Sir, Are we never to be satisfied? During the last year or two we have heard so many complaints about the dullness of cricket, the uninteresting and painful stonewalling, and the general 'decline' of our national game. ... our cricketers are once more ruining the game by their dull and lifeless methods!

> Sir, I am increasingly certain that there is too much County Cricket played, of too low a standard, to dwindling crowds. ... Things were better in my day.

> Sir, ... The whole concept of the county game has changed for the worse, with no midweek cricket, apart from some one-day matches, and no fixtures over the May Bank holidays. It just bears no reasoning.

Two of these extracts are from genuine letters to 'The Daily Telegraph' newspaper [2] and one is from the Tyers and Beach book, but can you tell parody from the real thing? Does it help to know that the telegraph quotes are from June, 1934 and July, 1994? If it doesn't, then the answer is that the second quote purports to be parody and the genuine newspaper quotes are arranged chronologically.

I wish this book was really an annual; it would be on my Christmas list. I do recommend 'W.G. Grace Ate My Pedalo', but forewarn potential readers that they need an appropriate and irreverent sense of humour to enjoy it as much as I.

[1] Tyers, A. and Beach (2010) *The Wisden Cricketer Presents 'W.G. Grace Ate My Pedalo': A Curious Cricket Compendium.* John Wisden & Co.

[2] Smith, M. (Ed.) (2011) *Not in My Day, Sir: Cricket Letters to The Daily Telegraph.* Aurum Press.

Chapter 12

Fingers and Thumbs.

Contrary to what you might expect from the title, this chapter is not about bowling. What it is about is numerology, and belief, and an impossible wish for the world to be a more rational place.

Trust me, the following is true. At several international science and engineering conferences, in front of hundreds, I have heard people stand up and refer to their ten fingers. I have never met anyone with ten fingers. I understand it can occur, but it is certainly uncommon[14].

My hands, in total, have ten digits, consisting of eight fingers, of four mirror image pairs, and two thumbs. In this, at least, I am distressingly normal. Thumbs are not the same as fingers. Thumbs have a greater range of movement than fingers and are usually described as 'semi-opposable', which is illustrated by not being able to touch the back of one's hand with that hand's thumb.

It is almost a shame that I am beyond atheism, holding no beliefs, religious or otherwise. It's a shame because our hands could be described as perfectly designed for the most rational counting system. Darwinian evolution and its related, subsequent theories posit no biological design, so the perfect arrangement of our fingers and thumbs for counting can only be put down to fortuitous chance.

[14] Apparently Sir Garfield Sobers was so born, but the extra fingers were surgically removed soon after birth. Widely suggested as the greatest all-rounder ever, even if they had worked, such additional fingers could hardly have improved his brilliant catching, but what it might have done for his bowling is impossible to estimate. His batting glove manufacturer would have had an "interesting" problem.

Unless one prefers to do one's arithmetic tediously using fractions, as people of my age were forced to do at school, then there are only two rational counting systems, octal and hexadecimal. Octal uses base eight counting and hexadecimal base sixteen. The idea of base eight counting is very simple, one just doesn't have the numbers eight and nine, so when counting one goes: 0, 1, 2, 3 ... 6, 7, 10, 11 ... 16, 17, 20 ... . Against hexadecimal is that it needs more than our standard ten number symbols and current convention is to use the capital letters A to F. Really against hex is that children would have to learn their times-tables up to 15 (F in hex), whereas with octal one doesn't need the decimal eight and nine times-tables to be able to multiply.

Octal is the rational choice for counting because any octal number can be very simply converted to binary and, *vice versa*, any string of binary noughts and ones can be immediately read out as an octal number. You can't do this with damned decimal; my laboratory in Cambridge bought me a very expensive calculator in the 1970s, over one hundred pounds, just so I could do decimal to octal conversions for my computer programming (my first laboratory computer didn't even have chips in it!). Binary is the logical minimum, the base to which all more complicated mathematics can be ultimately reduced. Against binary is that even small numbers need a lot of zeros and ones, hence octal, based on three binary bits, is the only rational choice for a counting system.

Our fingers are perfect for base eight, octal counting. Each finger represents a digit (1-7 and 0) and the thumbs are our counting device, pointing to each finger in turn. If it wasn't for those who can't tell their fingers from their thumbs, then perhaps, for once, the human race would have behaved sensibly and gone for octal counting.

What has any of this to do with cricket? The answer is really about runs and the importance placed on one hundred of them (and fifty). If the historical choice of choosing to count in decimal, base ten, was a poor, irrational one, then it is equally irrational to place much importance on the difference between 99 and 100 runs: decimal 99 is 173 octal and 100 is 174 octal; 100 octal is 64 decimal.

My Concise Oxford English Dictionary says numerology is "study of occult meaning of numbers", and occult there is defined as involving the supernatural, mystical and magical. There is nothing special about one hundred in decimal excepting when used in irrational base ten, so making any sort of fuss about a century of any type, for batsman or bowler, might fairly be described as numerology. In the more rational, Octal Universe, commentators would be saying things like, "He just didn't manage to reach his one hundred and seventy four runs." Of course, they wouldn't say this, but would transfer their excitement to 100, 200, 300 and 400 octal, 64, 128, 192 and 256 decimal respectively. I would still consider such excitement as numerology.

One would have more chance regularising English spelling, a *cause célèbre* amongst some literati such as G.B. Shaw of a hundred or so years ago, than ever moving to the sensible octal counting system. So, why wish for the impossible?

I am not wishing for the impossible. Accepted, we cannot change the decimal counting world, but we could change our attitude to it. This would be an example of what I call psychological engineering. Before I am unreasonably accused of cynical, manipulative Machiavellianism[15], however, a primary heuristic of my own psychological engineering is: Do not trust any psychological method that involves secrecy. In a nutshell, I tell you I'm going to change your mind, which you accept (because it is in your own best interests), and then I do. In any case, I'm allergic to penicillin and liars.

---

[15] I don't mind reasonable versions of such accusations, which I will happily and vigorously defend.

What we should all do is accept that 50 or 100 decimal are not special numbers, that any importance placed on them is numerology, and just stop making a fuss about it. A good place to start, because it's the largest target, would be cricket commentators in all media, including the tweeting general public. A sufficient, anti-numerology groundswell might then find rather smaller but perhaps more important targets.

Many, many times I have heard on live commentary comments about batsmen along the lines of, 'the selectors pay attention to three figures'. I think this is irresponsible if true, and I fear it might be. Oh what damage did 'Lord' Ted Dexter do when as an England selector he referred to "Malcolm Devon" (*ibid.*). To be very serious, over attention by selectors to batting tons could well cost someone their place in the team and significantly and negatively affect their whole career.

On the other side of the coin, the 'nervous nineties' is undoubtedly an issue with many batsmen because they too are under numerology's sway. It certainly does seem that for some that runs do dry up between decimal 90 and 100 and, with a concomitant change in batting style, they may also be expected to be more likely to lose their wicket.

Similarly, captains have often delayed a tactically desirable declaration so that a batsman can complete their hundred. It is impossible to tell, but some matches may have been won or lost because overs were lost pursuing a silly numerological target. A captain sensible enough to declare when batsman are near such targets has to be brave because, no matter how obvious are the tactical advantages of the declaration, inevitably there will be comment in dressing rooms, committees and in the media.

A common accusation against academics is that it is all very well being critical, but what would you replace it with? While I will maintain that it is a good academic's duty to disbelieve, in this instance I do have an answer to any accusers. What we want is a more sophisticated mathematical model and, I suggest, one that is relative. As a simple illustration, consider the following two cases: Batsman A makes 103 in an innings total of 515; Batsman B makes 67 in an innings total of 134. Batsman A may have made a ton, but they contribute a mere fifth of the team's runs; Batsman B makes half of his team's runs. Whatever the critical factors, the state of the wicket, quality of bowling, etc., it is hard to not give greater credit to Batsman B over A, but that is not how it will readily appear to most people once the match has gone and only the record books remain. The concept needed is 'relativity', that Batsman B performs better *relative* to Batsman A.

Cricket records were developed in a pre-computer age. Yes, any new, relativity based models will be more complicated, but this is a case of that-is-what-computer-are-for; they are very good at mathematics, if less so for just about anything else. I find it sad that live cricket commentators are still using bits of paper with Duckworth-Lewis Method outcomes tabulated. It should just be a software application (a.k.a. an app) on their PC, tablet or mobile phone. Let's have lots more apps so that cricket scores can be understood more rationally and in ways which take into account different performances in different matches or, even, different innings in the same match. For the computer literate live cricket commentator this would be a boon as it would give them even more to talk about, intelligently, rather than retreating into pre-scientific numerology.

Chapter 13

Entertaining the Entertainment Industry.

Without exaggeration, hundreds of times I have heard cricket commentators say that they are in the entertainment industry. I do not dispute this. Nor is this a recent claim. In March, 1971, John Arlott, writing in the Guardian explicitly states "and cricket is part of the entertainment industry" [1, p211]. This I will question, if not actually dispute.

What does Arlott mean by 'cricket' in the quote above?[16] The implication is that cricket is a thing and, if one can accept this, then it must be a very complex thing. I call such things 'systems'. Large, complex systems are made of many things of many different types. Some of these things are physical objects, demonstrably so by the bruises caused by cricket balls. Others are intangible, abstract things that cannot be touched. All psychological states fall into this latter category. Some things may be both, such as the spirit of cricket, which is both shared beliefs about how cricket should be played and, also, a physical, written document promulgated by ICC. The contents of the intangible beliefs and the physical document overlap, but are not identical, although the written form may be a subset of the belief system, i.e. everything in the written format is also in the shared beliefs, but not *vice versa.*

To give a simple example, the ICC's spirit of cricket document makes no mention of the Mankad, where a bowler runs out the non-striking batsman without bowling

---

[16] N.B. For simplicity's sake I deliberately finessed addressing this question in Chapter 10 and elsewhere.

the ball. Some commentators contend that this is always against the spirit of cricket, while more will agree that it is, if the bowler doesn't first warn the batsman about his backing up. In general systems analysis it is almost a hallmark of a large system that it can be seen from multiple perspectives: physical, psychological, financial, social, and so forth. In such a context, disagreement about what beliefs are shared about something like Mankading is quite a minor problem.

The 'Cricket System' is a vast mess. This is not necessarily a bad thing unless one were a general systems analyst tasked with modelling Arlott's cricket. Furthermore, with more limited aims, it is usually possible for the expert analyst to model only parts of a much larger system and, if one believes everything is connected to everything else, then this is what is only ever possible. I shall follow this approach, simplistically by my standards, when addressing the issue as to whether 'cricket' is part of the entertainment industry, and, if so, what sort of beast it is.

To start, the concept of industries used here might differentiate the entertainment industry from business, manufacturing, retail, government, health, military, IT, finance, and on and on, and, also, from the sports industry. Prototypical examples of the entertainment industry might be theatre, films, and concerts. The basic idea is that those in the entertainment industry deliver a show. Everyone in the industry is contributing in some way or form to the show, as are any things, stage, props, instruments, technology, that the show uses.

Clearly, actors and musicians are part of the entertainment industry, indeed, their *raison d'être* is to provide entertainment to their audience. Equally clearly, this is not so for the amateur cricket player. Evidence for this can be found in many books describing club cricket, many written by authors who admit to not being very good at the game, for example [2, 3]. One belief that is *not* in any of these books is that these duffers play so as to entertain a match's spectators, if there are any beyond WAGs[17], parents, progeny and a man walking his dog.

Is the situation much different for County cricket given their attendance figures? Attendances are even worse for a County second XI. The ECB have, of late, been working hard at "grass roots" levels, including school children, women's cricket and for the disabled. While there is, quite rightly, an emphasis on cricket being a sport played for fun, the ECB also provides a career structure for potential professional cricketers. Coming through a route in this development structure, the proto-pro cricketer will necessarily have played cricket as a sport. What they will never have done, except perhaps for their parents, is have played cricket so as to provide entertainment to anyone watching. Why should they change when in a County or Test side? I suspect most couldn't change, even if they had a lucrative ECB central contact that explicitly required them to play entertaining cricket.

Cricket professionals are sportsmen, or could be women, or transgender, and they play the game of cricket. Yes, each match is a show to those who attend, physically or electronically, but the players do not have the role of actors, they are not there to entertain the crowd but, individually and collectively, to play the game as well as they are able. As Ricky Ponting [4, p213] makes explicit, "for me it was always about what was going to give us the best chance to win rather than what might entertain the masses".

The 'Cricket System' needs to be modelled as having two distinct subsystems, one for sport and one for entertainment. There is communication and overlap

---

[17] No matter how gorgeous, no woman can be *a* WAG as the acronym stands for 'Wives And Girlfriends'. It's a collective noun, which unlike 'people' does not have an equivalent singular to 'person', for the obvious reason that someone is either a wife or a girlfriend. On the other hand, I'd be quite happy to introduce the beautiful Japanese wife as my "wife and girlfriend", which may explain the longevity of our marriage.

between these subsystems, which is complicated general systems analysis stuff beyond this chapter, but much that is in the sport subsystem is exclusive to it, as is so for the much larger entertainment subsystem. This logical separation of sport and entertainment is not mere academic posturing, for, once identified, it has an obvious practical implication in pointing to a common logical fallacy.

That cricket is not as good as it used to be, that it has become less entertaining, is a criticism that has been levelled at the game since, at least, late Victorian and Edwardian times, and has been, it seems, repeated down the generations, notwithstanding when the critics pitch their Golden Age of Cricket. Oft has been the cry for "Brighter Cricket!", but too often the proposed solutions involve the players. This is illogical. The players are in the sport subsystem and so are ill placed to solve an entertainment subsystem problem. Problems, if real, with cricket's entertainment value should be solved by those in its entertainment industry, so sensibly keeping problems and solutions within the same logical space.

To make the above concrete, below I briefly examine two classes of solution: (1) changing the rules and Laws; and (2) changing media commentary style. ICC, and national organisations, can fiddle with the rules and Laws of cricket with the aim of increasing cricket's entertainment values. I have devoted my life to learning how to think better and look on this game changing fiddling in woeful awe. A recent, popular nonsense amongst the hard of thinking has been the 'Law of Unintended Consequences'. The legislators are facing an almost impossible task, because it is a design task, which means it involves predicting possible futures, and what is being redesigned is the most complicated sport in the world.

Cricket, of course, is not as complicated as people, even cricket players are "beyond human ken" ([5] and *ibid.*). The players' views of the rules and Laws involve how these may be pushed to the advantage of their team, and themselves. It must be hard for the game change attempters to successfully anticipate all the ways the different players, along with their support staff, will react to changes when these legislators are focused on improving entertainment, rather than on the ways to win, or win a draw, playing cricket.

My second solution concerns the style of commentary provided by the live media formats, television, radio and the internet. I spent the early part of the English season of 2014 sampling BBC local radio ball-by-ball commentaries. While I'd say the quality of the ball-by-ball aspect of all the commentaries was pretty good[18], where they differed was in their other discussions throughout each match. Hard times for live commentators are in "slow passages of play" and when the match is "petering out to a draw". While banning these hackneyed phrases might seem desirous, it is the commentators' attitude behind them that might more usefully be adjusted. The commentators are part of cricket's entertainment industry and, as such, they have a duty to entertain their audience. This is difficult to achieve if commentators keep saying that the current play is boring.

Note, the above comment has nothing to do with the, often pre-emptive, commentators' defence that they have a duty to 'tell-it-as-they-see-it', even when this involves being highly critical of a player. Rather, it is about their duty to their audience and not to the players who are not part of the entertainment side of cricket. I'll happily admit that there are many excellent live cricket commentators who try very hard to be positive in entertainment adverse conditions. I still think it worth making the requirement explicit, that commentators should project a positive attitude, even unto 'positive spin' in the PR sense, otherwise, why should their audience continue to watch or listen?

---

[18] Excepting my standard complaint that I'm not reminded of the handedness of the batsmen often enough (Chapter 6).

I think those of us who do continue to follow a match, in spite of any 'it's-not-very-interesting' contrary advice, have the right of it. Boycott's Heuristic, look at the score and add two wickets, is a simple, good one for adding interest. I often spend my time in mental arithmetic, for example calculating targets to possible tactics at different run rates; it keeps me interested in the minutiae of a match (Chapters 14 and 23). Those less arithmetically adept in the audience might appreciate these and other interest maintaining devices being done for them.

Finally, what happens when a cricket match is played for the entertainment of those who attend physically or electronically? I was fortunate to have just such an example while I was first drafting this chapter. The 'Bicentenary Celebration Match' commemorated two hundred years of play at the third and still extant Lord's ground. It was played between MCC and Rest Of World (ROW) teams on Saturday 5th. July, 2014. The teams consisted of a galaxy of international stars, quite a few who had recently retired, although Brian Lara, bless him, was forty five years old by this time. I could see no reason for the allocation of players to teams, or was offered one by the MCC organiser in the pre-match build-up.

Shane Warne, captaining ROW won the toss and elected to bat. Interviewed after the toss, he said that "both were great teams" and that he hoped they'd "provide entertaining cricket". Captaining MCC, Sachin Tendulkar followed this up by saying they wanted to "entertain the people and play good cricket". So, the goal to entertain was clearly in the captains' minds. Also clearly, many people were looking forward to this match. Lord's holds around twenty eight thousand people and tickets were sold out within forty five minutes of going on sale. Presumably most of the paying public also expected to be entertained.

I wasn't greatly entertained. Perhaps this was because I'm not used to exhibition matches, where not only the result doesn't matter, but it doesn't really matter to the players, none of whom were playing for their team place or career, as might be happening in an otherwise slow Test or County cricket match. It certainly was slow and, if it had gone the full distance, then play would have extended into a ninth hour: MCC won at 296 for 3 in 45.5 overs.

Entertainment versus Sport? The crux came at 11:45, when the masterful mystery spinner Saeed Ajmal took his fourth wicket in three overs, stranding ROW on 58 for 5. Commentators' comments were "stop taking wickets" and, "Too good Saeed, you're too good mate." The commentators' concern was that it wouldn't be good if ROW were all out for about a hundred, and one explicitly asked whether Tendulkar should change bowlers for entertainment's sake. To the captain's credit, he did leave Ajmal on until just after noon, but I think he was taken out of the attack prematurely.

Is this what we could expect, regularly, if cricket were played for its entertainment value rather than as a sport? I think the answer must be 'Yes', although the match fixing for the sake of the supposed entertainment value could be quite subtle. I suppose some people might enjoy it, but, including myself, I hope not the majority of cricket's current followers.

I'm not convinced that professional, red ball cricket is entertainment deficient. Perhaps I am easily entertained. I am sure that if there is any entertainment improving to be done, then the problems are for those on the entertainment side of cricket to solve. Let the players play the sport of cricket and let us be cautious about rule changes, which should be to improve the game, perhaps making more equal the balance between bat and ball, and not as attempts to make the wonderful game of cricket more entertainingly wonderful.

[1] Allen, D.R. (Ed.) (1984) *Arlott on Cricket: His Writings on the Game.* Willow Books, Collins.

[2] Berkmann, M. (2005) *Zimmer Men.* Aurum.

[3] Morgan-Grenville, R. and Perkins, R. (2012) *Not out First Ball: The Art of Being Beaten in Beautiful Places.* Bene Factum Publishing.

[4] Ponting, R. (2013) *Ponting at the Close of Play.* HarperSport.

[5] Diaper, D. (1989) *Designing Expert Systems: From Dan to Beersheba.* in *Knowledge Elicitation: Principles, Techniques and Applications.* (Ed. Diaper, D), 15-46. Ellis Horwood.

Chapter 14

Running Heuristics.

If I wanted both to promote cricket and teach arithmetic to young school children, then I'd entertain them with a video recording of a cricket match and at points pause it so the children could do some useful sums. While I'm moderately good at mathematics, I'm pretty shaky at mental arithmetic, but I have got better in recent years because of my watching cricket on the radio. Deliberately, I don't use a calculator.

Why do I bother with all this mental arithmetic? I certainly do a lot of it, at times several calculations per over. Basically, I want to know how I think the session, day and match are progressing. I'm not sanguine about leaving this to the cricket commentators, indeed, I derive pleasure both from disagreeing with them and when they and I agree.

Doing the sums is just the first step. The results then need interpreting. What I have developed over the years is a set of heuristically derived targets, most, but not all concerning runs scored. A heuristic is a rule of thumb, something that is usually right but not always so (Chapter 10). Commonly used examples in cricket commentary is Geoffrey Boycott's 'Add two wickets and then how does the score look?' and, in fifty over games and usually attributed to Richie Benaud, 'At 30 overs, double the score to predict the 50 over one'[19].

Adding a note of caution, by the end of 2014 I'd heard a few commentators suggesting that the Benaud heuristic

---

[19] I've heard it suggested on cricket commentaries that Richie has a number of alternatives to the widely quoted one given here.

underestimated international scores due to rule changes, notably to do with fielding restrictions and players' eventual adaptation to them. In response, I've been testing the heuristic of whether a score a little shy of 150 in 25 overs works better.

People use many heuristics in their daily lives without realising what they are doing. Many of these heuristics don't involve mathematics, but I shall restrict this chapter's main considerations of heuristics to the subset that do. Unfortunately, many commonly used heuristics are poor. For example, laboratory experiments clearly show that people are poor at estimating probabilities and, more importantly, they are poor in consistent, predictable ways.

A key problem is how heuristics arise, where do they come from? There are always many answers to this question, but most are irrelevant to what I want here, which is to identify useful heuristics which will allow me to judge a match's progress. I do the mental arithmetic on the current state of a match so I can compare it to various heuristic targets.

What would appear to be a scientific approach to identifying useful targets would be to take a vast quantity of data from previous matches and to derive targets as 'measures of central tendency', commonly called "averages" by the general public and meaning the 'arithmetic mean'[20]. Some serious maths and statistics are needed. This is the approach adopted by the Duckworth-Lewis method and has the virtue of being public in that, if one has a suitable mathematical background, then the equations used are quite understandable. Duckworth-Lewis looks scientific and therefore is widely accepted as fair, although I have heard occasional grumbles of disquiet from commentary boxes.

I approve of the Duckworth-Lewis method while

[20] Divide X occurrences by N observations, e.g. 50 runs in 10 overs gives an arithmetic mean of 5 runs per over (50/10 = 5).

recognising that it could be improved, but, provided its data is regularly updated, then it is more than 'good enough for government' and quite a reasonable approach to use in cricket, particularly for its primary function of adjusting scores when overs are lost in limited overs cricket.

One measure is not enough for me. Really, you can't reduce the state of a match to a single number and why would one want to? To produce additional metrics to Duckworth-Lewis using the same approach is not feasible except by paid professionals with the computer resources to handle large volumes of disparate data, which needs serious database and programming skills. There is, however, another way.

In software engineering a heuristic analysis is one arrived at by one or more experts, for example, for requirements analysis or for testing things like functionality and usability[21]. I've done a lot of this in my professional career, mainly concentrating on the complex interactions between people and machines. I have used a similar heuristic approach to deriving and refining various cricket metrics over the last couple of decades.

Cricket commentators do it all the time. Before ordering the tee-shirt, the 'it' is to make a heuristic assessment of the current state of play in a cricket match. They do this at the drop of a hat, on the fly, using gut feeling, intuition and so forth. What they really do is to access their vast, memorised experience and analysis of cricket and apply this to the current situation. How the mind does this is so vastly complicated that it should boggle the mind, it boggles mine as a psychologist, but even the minds of cricket commentators, who will admit to being "mathematically challenged", manage with consummate skill, unrecognised by such mind's owners. What they are doing is a heuristic analysis.

I've been doing the same, but what I've concentrated

[21] What it does and how easy and learnable it is for people.

on is using such a heuristic analysis during cricket matches to try and establish targets that reflect whether a passage of play is good, average or poor, mostly with respect to the batting side. Over the years I've been evaluating these targets, testing them during each match and refining the numbers.

Chapter 23 covers in some details my run-a-ball (rab) metric, but in red ball cricket my most used, because it is so useful, and simple, is my Doing Well Score (DWS) measure. I judge that a team is doing well, not brilliantly but better than average, when they achieve the following scores: 126-2, 155-3, >200-4. If these figures seem overly precise, well I've spent many, many hours, and still do, agonising whether it should be 126, 127 or 128 runs for two wickets. It doesn't really matter but a single number needs choosing just so one can do the subsequent sums.

To give examples of how I use DWS, say a team is 100-2, then they are 26 runs short of their DWS score (126 – 100). If they were 100-3 then they are a wicket short and are short of 55 runs from their DWS third wicket score of 155. Also, they are still 26 runs short of their second wicket target. At a higher level of analysis, if a batting side is well short of the DWS score, then this could be due to the nature of the wicket, poor batting, or good bowling and fielding, or a combination of these. The point is that one needs some measure of performance such as DWS before one attributes causation for poor, or good, performances.

I don't have similar, heuristically derive figures for the first and later wickets because I've found the variability of data across many matches too great for me to settle even for a range figure. This doesn't really matter as the opening overs of an innings can still be related to the 126-2 second wicket DWS target, and the first 200 runs usually determines how well, overall, an innings will go.

I've used DWS for fifty overs cricket and it works quite well, even though it makes no consideration of overs bowled and hence ignores the run rate. For this reason the figures used for DWS are not useful for judging Twenty20 matches.

I also have a red ball morning session DWS measure. If they are doing well, then a batting side with most of their wickets intact should get 108 runs in the morning session, ideally with the loss of no more than two wickets. I expect higher session scores after lunch and in the, usually longer, final session, unless wickets are lost quickly.

I also have a load of rather rougher heuristics which I suspect many people share with me. I expect a run a minute to be scored and that an over will take approximately four minutes[22]. Very roughly, I expect four runs an over in red ball cricket, six an over in fifty overs matches, and nine an over in Twenty20. Gratifyingly, and with relief, jotting down these number together for the first time when preparing this chapter allowed me to do some cross checking, and it works, they add up, thank goodness. If, on average, an over takes four minutes and four runs are scored from it, then that is one run a minute, which is what I claimed to expect.

I've also DWS heuristics for the limited overs' power plays. For the first power play I've DWS targets of 56 runs in ten overs and 47 in six overs, for fifty overs and Twenty20 matches, respectively. The Twenty20 target was directly derived from the Australian Big Bash competition of 2013 and, a year later, I've some indications that it is already too low. I intend further research to confirm this suspicion before I speculate as to possible reasons for such a change, if it has occurred.

Finally, there are two heuristics that I've found very useful and that I've used for years. First, to evaluate a batsman's innings, what percentage of runs are scored in

---

[22] In County cricket, where points can be lost for slow over rates, the official required over rate is 3mins:45secs – 32 overs per two hour session. Over rates in Test matches tend to be lower, i.e. overs take longer to bowl than in County games.

boundaries? My estimate is that in a well constructed red ball innings about half the runs should be scored in boundaries. This heuristic works reasonably well in fifty over cricket, perhaps preferring a shade above the 50% mark, but not in the Twenty20 game. To boorishly stress a point, this heuristic target is for a "well constructed" innings which is not the same as an average calculated from previous matches.

My other, developed long ago and still frequently used, heuristic concerns extras. I developed it from watching, on radio or television, red ball cricket and I've not developed a similar one for the white ball games, although I use my red ball one with a large ladle of generosity to take into account the vicious leg side wide rule in the fifty overs game. The measure involves the percentage of an innings total that is scored as extras. I judge a team using the following numbers: Excellent – less than 4%; Good – 4-7%; Acceptable – 7-9%; Poor – 9-12%; Terrible – anything over 12%. Ignoring low scoring innings where 'Extras' is listed as nearly the best batsman, I've found that this heuristic can provide quite subtle insights into a team's bowling and fielding performance when the source of a large numbers of extras is also examined, no balls versus wides, for example.

During every match I am always also doing calculations on the fly, trying to find ways to evaluate the current situation and thus evaluate possible tactics, strategies and outcomes. It is from this that I've developed my heuristics so that I need to do fewer sums and so get to see more cricket.

My example heuristics above are not intended to be exhaustive. I have others and, for sure, other people have ones that I don't use. My purpose has been to expose some of the heuristics that I have deliberately developed over the years so that other people might develop their own; they will do so anyway, unconsciously, but as a psychologist I've always thought that making thought explicit, public even unto oneself, is itself a valuable exercise and an essential precursor to rational thinking.

A heuristic analysis is one done by one or more experts. Experts do disagree. People are welcome to dispute the numbers I've given above, I hope it gives them as much pleasure as it does me, trying to make them better. As long as my figures are in the right ball park, then I really don't mind, and not long after publication some of my figures will no doubt have to change as cricket evolves, by rule changes or different approaches to playing the great game. We are in a Red Queen's race, running to stand still, which guarantees a possible lifetime of interest in, and hopefully interesting, cricket.

Chapter 15

Watching One Match on the Radio.

Watching cricket on the radio isn't like watching it visually, at the ground or on television. So I had the brainwave of giving my readers a match report of my radio watching of a match. I thought it would be a very different beast from a normal match report which is normally produced by someone who was at the ground, although I believe there is occasional, scurrilous gossip that some reporters fake it from the television. I also thought it would be very hard work. No, I wasn't surprised that both these thoughts turned out to be correct. I made arrangements with other people, including the beautiful Japanese wife and The Daughter, on Monday that I could not be disturbed after 10 o'clock from Tuesday to Friday, that I was busy with work that involved interactive real-time multimedia and would not answer the telephone or the door.

Which match to report on? It was early September, 2014, and there were just three rounds of County Championship matches remaining. After this I faced England's red ball desert where, because of the World Cup in early 2015, England would play none of the longer form until the following spring. I thought it had to be red ball, because the limited overs games lack the strategic and tactical complexity of the longer forms because they just don't have the playing time. September in England can be a glorious time of year, but the weather isn't guaranteed, so if were to be done, it had best be done swiftly.

It would be the Durham match because Martin Emmerson of BBC Radio Newcastle had been the best commentator using email that I'd found, being both swift and reliable. In addition, I'd enjoyed the most marvellous match of the season the previous week at the Riverside, Chester-le-Street, where Durham had beaten Nottinghamshire and commentators with Martin had been two of the three Daves, Townsend (DT) and Bracegirdle, both favourite, excellent commentators. My qualm was that Durham's opponents would be Middlesex and at Lord's Kevin Hand often reported that his email there was iffy to non-existent. It was for this reason that, much as I love DT's commentary, I'd switched from following Middlesex to Durham earlier in the year.

Middlesex and Durham were sixth and seventh in the County Championship table and both were on 150 points. Northamptonshire, on 64 points, would be relegated to Division Two and, probably, Lancashire on 138. Middlesex or Durham could still be relegated. A win for either side would prevent this and a draw with plenty of bonus points would probably make both sides safe from relegation.

The morning of Tuesday, 9th. September, 2014 was a lovely, mostly sunny, autumn day, but it did not start well for BBC local radio. Until dead on 10:30 all both my computers could get was a looped voice message, "Thank you for choosing to listen to BBC radio ... Unfortunately the current programme is unavailable ... due to contractual reasons or a temporary technical fault ...".

Then, came the voice of Kevin Hand, talking of the greenest of Lord's wickets and that under such circumstances Middlesex's Tim Murtagh was as good a bowler as anyone in England. My digital clock turned over to 10:31 and I discovered that Kevin was discussing this because the score was that Durham, who had won the toss and elected to bat on this green Lord's wicket, were 1 for 1. Murtagh had bowled Keaton Jennings, between bat and pad to hit middle and leg stumps, second ball, for a golden duck. At the end of the first over, Durham were 5 for 1.

I sent my previously prepared email of greetings. I sent

it to Martin Emmerson's address given Hand's known technical difficulties at Lord's. A quarter of an hour into the match, Kevin gave out the Middlesex email address as the one to use, so I resent my greetings which Martin read out in his Dr. Dan voice at 10:54[23]. Alas, this was to be, with one exception, the only email that would be read out that Tuesday.

Middlesex, as they should, set an attacking field with three slips and gully. With England's six month hiatus of red ball cricket, I wondered whether any of them would remember how to field at second and third slip by the Spring of 2015. I always prefer my cricket with slips. Finn bowled from the other end. He'd spent the 2014 season playing to recover his form and for his England place after being deemed "unselectable" during the Winter's Ashes tour in Australia. By 11 o'clock, Finn was bowling to a 6:3 field.

The headline cricket story of the day was that Saeed Ajmal had been banned for an illegal bowling action. Mention was made of how he'd nearly ruined the Lord's Bicentenary match earlier in the year (see Chapter 13). That it had taken nearly all season, it was speculated, might not reflect well on umpires, or as I thought, the system within which national and international umpires must operate. DT shouted from the back of the commentary box that, "He was a dead man walking."

Watching the cricket on the radio was somewhat interrupted as Kevin Hand spent seven minutes muttering of his password problems until he "Got it!" at 10:54, my email was read out, and, in the same minute, Durham were

---

[23] Early in the 2014 County season I'd been dubbed "Dr. Dan" by several commentators when reading emails from me. Following Durham for the second half of the season, because I appreciated Martin Emmerson's commentary so much, Martin took to reading out my emails in his "Dr. Dan voice", which was subsequently noted and discussed by other commentators. I was flattered by the voice, deep, calm and reasonable (I think) and to which I emailed that it "sounded more like me than I do".

20 for 2 in the fifth over. Tim Murtagh, again, this time taking Mark Stoneman, caught behind, for 4 runs after twenty minutes. A disaster for Durham as Stoneman had provided impressive, much needed stability to Durham's openers during the season. Commentary consensus was that Durham were wrong to choose to bat and that if Middlesex had won the toss, they would have put Durham in. They seemed right as after half an hour of play Murtagh was 3 for 16 in the seventh over and Durham were 24 for 3 having lost Richardson on four, caught at second slip by Dawid Malan. It would have gone to third man in a limited overs game, and probably for four given widespread, much commented on, general reluctance by teams to push third man back.

The commentary team were, to mix metaphors, out of the blocks and flying down the wing from the first tee. Even in the first hour, David Townsend had found fine mid-season form, on 1960s Playfair Book ties, apparently looking like green corduroy; and with a joke he'd given to John Carr, that Carr had scored a century coincident with the birth of his (Carr's) daughter, thus proving the adage that, "When you've got kids, you don't get out much." DT also, effortlessly, showed what makes him one of the best technical commentators on radio, wondering whether Tobias (Toby) Roland-Jones couldn't cut a couple of paces off his run up, although admitting that TRJ gets good rhythm at the crease from his long run in. Near noon, Martin Emmerson had Roland-Jones "running in from Paddington", and DT claiming, "I can't *bear* comments like that.", and more Paddington Bear marmalade related comments ensued until DT's usual sidekick, Kevin Hand, joined him at noon, three quarters of the way through the first session.

The corpsing Kevin Hand. He started with the suggestion that the commentary team were being irreverent to what was, after all, a serious relegation battle. "What, you mean like bringing Ollie Rayner on to bowl?", says DT. Collapse of the un-stout party. Kevin had a

Johnners and Aggers leg-over moment (famous, *ibid.*, and on YouTube) and was helpless with laughter for two or three minutes, and was still chuckling nearly ten minutes later. Ever the professional, DT took over the ball-by-ball commentary, no mere "throwaway comment" of his stopping a master, notwithstanding the odd chuckling gloat of sympathetic triumph at young Hand.

Rayner had come on to bowl and, while Kevin corpsed, Durham were 79 for 3 after 21 overs with, I thought, 27 minutes to lunch, so they had continued their healthy, four an over, run rate throughout the morning despite the loss of three early wickets. I usually reckon that a run a minute as a standard so I predicted Durham, if not losing a wicket, would be over the hundred before lunch, perhaps on 105. I was taking the match seriously and Durham did a bit better than my prediction, reaching, I think, 116 for 3 in 29 overs at lunch. Ollie Rayner may have been the butt of DT's joke, but in the afternoon DT described him as Middlesex's second best bowler of the day, after, of course, Tim Murtagh and his 24 for 3 early wickets.

An excellent morning's commentary and some reasonably good cricket. Ten minutes after noon I had the thought that the pitch had flattened out and the same thought occurred to DT a minute later. I do so like beating the pundits to such analyses. We all agreed two things from the session. First, Middlesex hadn't bowled well enough and would be disappointed at not getting more wickets after the first three cheap ones. On the other hand, DT had helpfully pointed out at quarter past twelve that at 95 for 3 after 25 overs, Middlesex had not conceded a single extra, which is extraordinarily expedient. Second, with Scott Borthwick and Ben Stokes at the crease for most of the morning, they ran many a chancy single, I counted about half a dozen. Any of these could have been a run out. I'm not sure how much blame can be attached to the Middlesex fielding, but these singles seemed foolish and unnecessary to me, even though generally I approve of batsmen rotating the strike.

Niggles from me on the morning was first the lack of email. I'd really wanted to ask Martin Emmerson about the bonus payments to the top County sides; he mentioned at 11:33 that coming third was worth £87,000. Second, my standard big niggle (see Chapter 6), which is probably a naggle, that they won't remind me whether batsmen are right or left handed. By my reckoning it was after twelve thirty before DT casually mentioned that it was Borthwick who was left handed. Third, that the outside microphone was turned off immediately at the start of lunch whereas, via email, Martin and I had agreed at an earlier match that it was much better for such to be left on during intervals. It lets me feel I'm at the ground and, critically, that the BBC local radio servers are still working.

How often following Middlesex have I started a session with the exhortation, "Come on, come on, young Kevin!" Mr. Organised, leave-it-till-the-last-second Hand, commenced commentary at 13:08 as Finn bowled the first ball. Very consistent, Kevin, but the ball's gone and I've no idea of how the field was set for it.

So the afternoon session on the radio then has a flurry of cricket and weather context, it's now sunny after some cloud had "filled in" in the morning. There are lunch time tweets but no emails and Kevin is apologising again for this lack within the first quarter hour. There's dull IT tech talk and Martin offers to give Kevin the number to ring, but nothing ever eventuates from this throughout the day.

Durham more than plug on, reaching 138 for three after just over half an hour. Interspersed with the cricket is a long discussion about which England players are being rested and not allowed to play some County matches in September. I share Kevin's disgust and can but agree with his irony that, in its wisdom, ECB deem that their seam bowlers need a full six weeks rest before England tour Sri Lanka. "Six Weeks!" Finn's a bowler who needs to bowl and he's not allowed to bowl in Middlesex's last two County matches, and he's hardly played for England all season. The ECB? *Plus ça changé, plus c'est la même chose*, "the more something apparently changes, the more it essential remains the same" [1].

Just after half past one Kevin signs off his stint with a guilty, "We did try to get some cricket in this morning." His leaving allows DT in collusion with Martin to return to meteorology and astronomy, whether it is the sun or the Earth which is moving and while they eventually agree that the planet orbits the sun, they are only partially right in stating that the sun doesn't move, missing the critical word, 'relative'; our sun and its solar system together are whizzing through space, relative to our galaxy, which is whizzing along relative to other galaxies. DT is actually referring back to a match with Kevin much earlier in the season and is now criticising Kevin, of whom he says claims that "the sun has moved behind the clouds" and that, correctly, "We're in trouble if it has."

Well over a dozen years previously I decided to experiment with being more correct than common usage and eschew all reference in my utterances that the sun 'rose in the East' or 'moved across the sky'. It is harder than one might think to instead say, and think, that the planet I'm on is spinning Eastwards. What a pity there was no email, but, even if we were at this match towards the farcical end of cricket commentary, no other sport offers such opportunities for digression and consequent entertainment. As one tweet asked, "Have you been using banned substances?", but as Martin confesses, "No, we'd pass the test", pause, "but not the daftness test." Ben Stokes, who had recently started playing for England, and Scott Borthwick batted on, having reached 141 for 3 after 37 overs after starting together at 24 for 3; not a bad over rate really, I think, a tad under four an over (3.8), which DT comments on at about ten to two when the sums are easier (161 for 3 after 40 overs).

Cricket commentary continues when Kevin returns at 2 o'clock, that Middlesex have lost out after their three early morning wickets and should have taken at least two more before lunch. That in the season, Middlesex's bowlers haven't regularly performed as well as should be expected, unlike their batting, and that the bowling hasn't been good enough today, that they've bowled a lot of long hops, which were not slow ball bouncers (see Chapter 8). I check the current County Championship table and, indeed, Middlesex have 31 batting and 32 bowling points whereas Durham, with three wins to Middlesex's four, have 33 batting and 34 bowling points. So descriptively the commentators have a point, but I have doubts that analytically the difference is statistically significant, but I know of no way to calculate this.

In similar vein the afternoon progresses, between balls and overs discussion of the current match, the state of the Championship, mixed with tweets, and jokes old and new; Martin's next door neighbour was recently in some 'House Swap' television programme which leads to discussing what else other than houses might be swapped. At 3 o'clock Stokes is out for 85, bowled by the left arm spinner Neil Dexter, caught by wicket keeper John Simpson; Middlesex are 206 for 4 after 55 overs. Towards tea I notice that there are now no slips and while new batsman Collingwood is nearly out, or he played a "well controlled shot" to the last ball before tea, as DT summarised, "This session is coming to a sedate end."

With perfect timing my colleague of a quarter of a century, Colston Sanger, arrives at the tea interval with Middlesex on 226 for 4. The beautiful Japanese wife has made fresh, sticky ginger cake for Colston and at the start of the final session we repair upstairs so we can chat while the cricket commentary trickles on at low volume. Colston leaves at 5 o'clock, the new ball is taken, and two wickets fall in two overs: Collingwood out LBW to Murtagh's arm ball for 59; Muchall LBW to Finn for a duck. DT describes it as a "typical Finn ball" which "pitches just outside of off stump and nips back in to middle". He continues that if he'd a pound for every time he's seen it, then one could have a very nice meal out, but with whose wife is the subsequent question.

Consistent commentary continues. A tweet suggests there are "an astonishing number of topless men in the stand below you" (the commentator's box). DT and Kevin decide they need a nickname for "Marty" and ask listener's for suggestions, expecting the scurrilous. Asked what was his nickname at school, Martin Emmerson replies "Emma", to which DT observes, "That was before the operation."

Enough! The purpose of this chapter was to give my readers a taste of what it is like, for me, to watch cricket on the radio. I still have three more pages of handwritten notes, of the sixteen I made during the first day, which I have not used, but enough should be enough.

Except, and don't trust academics the first time they say they're finished, I had planned to cover all four days of the match. On the other hand, not one of Kevin's, good planning should anticipate contingencies and have sets of well prepared back-up plans. I always do and I had.

Commentary on day two, Wednesday, 10th. September, 2014, starts with the first ball with Durham on 348 for 7: Borthwick 169; Hastings on nought. It also pretty much starts with Martin Emmerson laughing at something DT says off air and within five minutes Martin is reading a long email about tests on different thickness of seat padding at Lord's, in his "Dr. Dan voice". Five minutes later he reads the first of the real Dr. Dan emails, of extreme sycophancy, DT attributes it to Martin's mum. The whole day is extremely jolly, from the commentators, tweeters and emailers, including several more from and about the author. I hope the tweet that "Dr. Dan's Diaries – worth a million there" turns out to be accurate. The whole day is rather like the Victoria and Albert Museum, a great café with a nice museum attached, or here, a wonderful, hilarious commentary with a nice game of cricket going on.

Middlesex have their traditional Middle Order Batting Collapse (MOBC) and are all out for 276 giving Durham a 101 run lead. Durham finish the day at 44 for 1.

For the hubris of the author's emails strikes Nemesis that evening. Martin had asked for a thirty second mp3 file of the real voice of Dr. Dan. Not something I'd done for ages, I had to download some software. Bang! Albeit a software 'Bang!' Operating system corrupted. Panic! Our lodger, Hannah, and I will spend nearly thirty hours rebuilding my main PC from the operating system up. Hannah keeps going until 1am and I start on it again at 5am. It will be over a fortnight before the system is fully restored.

Fortunately, days three and four focus on the cricket match, which is not to say they don't have their humorous moments, many actually, but, PC traumatised, I'm glad it's less like the V&A Museum. The final day looks like it will be a classic style of red ball cricket win, and so it turns out to be. It doesn't start so well for the BBC, there is no local radio commentary for the first 25 minutes of play. Middlesex need 395 to win and are one wicket down. I point out in an email that this is only four runs an over. Middlesex, however, only go for the conservative strategy and then they might "go for a dart", says DT, near the end, if they still have wickets in hand. By lunch they don't, being 139 for 7, losing Malan LBW to Captain Collingwood on the last ball before the interval. "I don't want to put the mockers on him for the last ball.", the Townsend curse strikes. Durham win by 141 runs at 14:36. My pen runs out of ink as I record my final notes.

[1] Buchanan-Brown *et al.* (1980) *Le Mot Juste: A Dictionary of Foreign and Classical Words and Phrases.* Kogan Page.

Chapter 16

Hawkeye Needs Better Graphics.

On and on they go, the airwaves filled with commentator confusion about Hawkeye and the Decision Review System (DRS). For commentators Hawkeye should be a boon, meaning a gift or blessing, and what I would hope for is boon commentary, meaning congenial or jolly.

My impression is that it is ex-bowlers who are most to blame, which I generalise and paraphrase them as saying, “If the ball is hitting the stumps, then it is out.” Such utterances are made when Hawkeye shows on its graphics that less than half its projected ball is hitting the outer stumps or the bails. This situation is classified as ‘umpire’s call’, that is, the same ball would get the batsman out or not out consistent with the on-field umpire’s original decision. This can be viewed as no bad thing.

Hawkeye, developed by Dr. Paul Hawkins and first used in 2001, is a clever system that uses multiple cameras, usually six, located high above the ground. I always thought that the technically difficult bit was tracking the ball automatically and that once this was solved, all the rest was mere trigonometry[24], a subject I was taught thoroughly at school long before I’d turned sixteen and which can be easily coded by any half decent computer programmer. This is not to denigrate Hawkeye’s software which must be huge to cope with the real vagaries of a cricket ball’s movement through the air, its spin and so forth, if it is to achieve its claimed accuracy, according to

[24] The mathematics of triangles involving the length of sides and size of angles.

Wikipedia, of two tenths of an inch (0.5cm).

Adding a predictive capacity to Hawkeye just involves more of the same programmed mathematics. So, if the ball's flight from where it pitched to the wicket is interrupted by the batsman in a Leg Before Wicket (LBW) situation, then the ball's unimpeded trajectory can be predicted by Hawkeye. Such flight interruptions are likely to be only a matter of a couple of yards between batsman and wicket, so an error of half a cricket ball, which has a radius about 1.4 inches, is more than generous with respect to Hawkeye's predictive capabilities[25].

The BCCI's objection to using Hawkeye's predictive capabilities is ludicrous, although entirely consistent with much of its other recent behaviours as, for example, described in detail by Gideon Haigh [1]. Being consistent, however, can be vice rather than virtue and in my own field of Human-Computer Interaction (HCI), which is the study of everything to do with people and digital technologies, then the concept of 'foolish consistency' in user interfaces has at times proved useful. In this sense, Haigh opens one chapter thus: "Say what you like about members of the ICC, they are utterly consistent. No matter how far you lower your expectations, they always find a way to underperform." (p237). This is mild compared to some of his criticisms of ICC and, he claims, its *de facto* boss, BCCI.

That India refuses to play international cricket with Hawkeye or other DRS technologies such as the snickometer and hotspot (see Chapter 5) is illogical, even if they had a reasonable technical case against Hawkeye predictions, which they don't. If ICC were not in thrall to India's financial might within international cricket, then they might instruct their elite panel of umpires to forego

---

[25] Law 5 (The Ball) actually specifies the weight and circumference of a new ball (813/16 to 9 inches or, metrically, 22.4 – 22.9cm). As a circle's circumference = $2\pi r$, then the radius (r) is simply $9/2\pi$.

the traditional batsman's advantage when the on-field umpire is in doubt and give the beneficial decision to the non-India team who would otherwise use DRS; giving the benefit of doubt to batsmen is not part of the Laws of cricket. How long could the BCCI hold out if they lost three or four wickets in every international match because they refused to use DRS?

Prediction is built into the Laws of cricket for LBW decisions as the on-field umpires must decide whether the ball would have hit the stumps when all the other criteria are met (e.g. batsman hit in line and the ball pitched in line for leg stump deliveries, and the batsman was playing a shot). The issue is who or what is able to make better predictions, an unaided umpire or one assisted by DRS technologies, particularly Hawkeye.

The consensus view amongst cricket's pundits, perhaps outside of India at least, seems to be that improving umpiring decisions is beneficial. In the pro-DRS camp, I recommend Phil Tufnell's summary [2, pp367-373]. The more rational anti-technologists of a few years ago seem mostly won over, that the on-field umpires' authority has not been catastrophically undermined, although far more LBW decisions are given out since DRS was introduced, and, as the technologies have become more efficient, DRS does not greatly interrupt the flow of play. I've always liked DRS, even when it was slower, and I like my own, real-time judgements confirmed, or not, so I can learn, that the ball was missing off stump, was too high, outside the line of leg stump, etc.

Much more importantly, and in this too rare instance I agree with the ICC, that DRS is supposed to be used to prevent very poor umpiring decisions, also known as "howlers". That this is often not how teams use it should be no surprise and there is plenty of boon commentary to be enjoyed in discussions on the DRS tactics of captains. What is to be enjoyed less are the comments, paraphrased above, that if according to Hawkeye the ball is hitting the stumps, then the batsman is out. This view requires that

Hawkeye is 100% accurate at predicting a single future, which is as illogical as it is impossible. It is also against the Laws of cricket as a batsman is not out when his stumps are struck, but only if the bails are dislodged. A very fine nick of the stumps doesn't allow Hawkeye to predict that the bails would come off, and occasionally they lift and resettle on the stumps, which is not out.

The problem with the hundred percenters is that they treat the exact location of the edge of the ball as shown on Hawkeye as a single, assumed real, future. It may be a very good guess by Hawkeye, but it is only a guess. My design suggestion is that these commentators' problem could be nearly eradicated, not by changing Hawkeye, but by changing its visual user interface. What Hawkeye currently displays is a predicted cricket ball's location in relation to a stump's or bail's location. In my redesign what would be shown would be the centre of the ball and a haze of probability around this.

In simplistic terms, my Hawkeye's ball would have a central spot, say in red, and this would gradually fade out towards the ball's perimeter. In consequence, the edge of the ball would be invisible and the point of this style of display would be to remind viewers that Hawkeye cannot be error free.

In less simplistic terms, there are a number of further design options that need to be considered. For example, unless Hawkeye can provide a different statistical model of its locational error, then the fade from centre to periphery would be Normal, that is, bell shaped, so that the area of the ball around halfway between it's centre and periphery would fade rapidly whereas near the middle and edge the fade would be very gradual. Additionally, would showing the edge of the ball as a hard line defeat the purpose of the redesign, to stop treating Hawkeye's predictions as totally accurate?

Related to the above, and perhaps less obvious, is how large should Hawkeye's graphic ball be? With the present solid ball graphic the ball is the size of a cricket ball relative to the stumps. With the redesigned graphic the ball could be any size, although the maximum would probably be limited to the current third umpire's rule that more than half the Hawkeye ball must be hitting wicket or bail to be out. Such a double sized Hawkeye ball would have a diameter of five and three quarter inches and to viewers there would still be some, albeit quite faded, part of the ball visibly overlapping the target.

Yet another option on ball size would be to use Hawkeye's claimed accuracy, which if it is a fifth of an inch either way, would give the Hawkeye graphic ball a diameter of about three and a third inches, i.e. about 12% wider than a ball's actual, relative to the stumps, size.

This is an instance where what is needed is not mere design, but empirical testing, which is the job of applied psychologists working in the field of cognitive ergonomics. That's me! .. or my colleagues in this field. Quite a lot of different experiments could be carried out. The simplest are probably aesthetic, measuring what viewers are most comfortable with across a range of designs. The difficult experiments to design are functional testing ones, establishing how large should be the Hawkeye ball that minimises viewers being certain of a hit wicket in close situations. Such experiments are extremely complicated and are difficult to design to meet international standards of scientific rigour as they will probably have to train subjects first, giving them appropriate perceptual beliefs. There are lots of other experimental design complications, for example, involving laboratory simulation fidelity, of the environment, stimuli and subject sampling.

Physics, chemistry, biology and experimental psychology are all classed as hard sciences, but in comparison, the first three are easy compared to experimental psychology, which I believe is the most difficult science humans have ever attempted. I thought that as a teenager and after forty years of doing it I am convinced it is so. 'Rocket Science', which is really mostly engineering and philosophically quite different from science, is trivially easy compared to scientific psychology. I could design the experiments outlined above, but it is a job for specialist scientists.

To reiterate and so stress, my redesign of Hawkeye's visual presentation of the ball would not change umpiring decisions at all as the same criterion from the software, that at least half the ball is striking stump or bail, would still apply and can be simply conveyed to the umpire by a binary state, say a red or green light. The fancy graphics are for public consumption, for entertainment's sake. Improving the graphics would certainly improve my own entertainment if it stopped, or even reduced significantly, silly commentary that is over deterministic. For those who believe because they've seen it with their own eyes, 'Calm down dear, it's only a computer simulation.'

[1] Haigh, G. (2010) *Sphere of Influence: Writings on Cricket and Its Discontents.* Simon & Schuster UK.

[2] Tufnell, P. and Barnes, J. (2012) *Tuffers' Cricket Tales*. Headline.

Chapter 17

Speaking of English.

England's six month international red ball cricket hiatus of 2014-15 was nigh upon me. On the Monday before the start of the final rounds in the County Championship the following day, I decided I'd get in a little white ball cricket training. What was on was on Pakistani television (PTV). I would watch the Bahawalpur Stags versus the Abbotabad Falcons in the Haier Cup Twenty20 competition at the National Stadium Karachi. Streaming PTV to my own television was remarkably reliable; in over three hours the stream dropped out only a couple of times and was easily reloaded.

In honesty I don't recall much of the match, I became distracted. What first caught my attention in the early overs of the first innings was a use of "unique" that was entirely new to me. I am an embarrassed monolingual. French totally beat me at all my four grammar schools. Well I've rehearsed my memories of my first lesson, a gowned master entered the classroom and we all stood in a clatter of wood and cast iron from our Victorian desks. "Good Morning, Sir", I mumbled as we had been taught, but it was only after the cacophony of the class reseating had died down that I realised that something strange was going on. The master was talking, but I couldn't understand a word he was saying. Everyone else seemed to have some sort of a clue, except me. I never recovered, even after school, private lessons didn't help. In retrospect, I didn't know what was a verb in English so couldn't relate all those French verb lists into any English equivalent. I've been with the beautiful Japanese wife for over thirty years. I tried to learn Japanese that long ago with even less success than with French. As an embarrassed monolingual I have only respect for those with the gift of tongues.

I do not criticise non-native English speakers who gamely struggle with English's numerous types of inconsistency, of pronunciation, spelling and, particularly, grammar. A good, lay summary may be found in Bill Bryson's 'Mother Tongue' [1] and I commend his point (p128) that the attempt by Classicists to straightjacket extant English into Latin grammar was as foolish as it has been unsuccessful. In any case, a lot of it is about style rather than communication. For example, when Booth points out that "the use and abuse of definite articles in Indian English is one of its most characteristic quirks" [2, p226], it does not hinder the understanding of his own example, "Also the physiotherapist of English team enjoyed squash game and lunch at Hotel Sayaji.", and they did manage to get in the first 'the'.

I do criticise native English English speakers. Years ago the beautiful Japanese wife and I competed as to who could spot the most times someone on television said "at this moment in time" when they simply meant 'now'. Of late my ire has been towards my countrymen's use of 'unique', which is an absolute, so utterances such as something being "fairly unique", "nearly unique" or, even, "uniquely unique" are to be scorned. If 'rare' is too rare then there are plenty of longer alternatives for the prolix, such as 'infrequent', 'unusual' or 'uncommon', which can be modified.

Back in Pakistan, during the early part of the Stags versus Falcon's match, noting that even their team names are English, the commentators were discussing how while the local Pakistani teams had numbers on the back of their uniforms, it would be more helpful if they used players' names as this would help their global audience more readily identify "players unique to them"; 'unique' is not any sort of synonym for 'unknown' or 'unfamiliar'.

In the normal course of things I wouldn't bother to

mention such semantic, if erroneous, creativity by a non-native English speaker as they are infinitely better at English than I am at any language other than English. It was as I was musing on this, however, that I suddenly realised that the match's commentary was no longer in English.

I hadn't noticed the switch immediately. Was this odd? I still had the video stream and television commentary is very different from radio's, adding to what can be seen on the screen rather than having to describe what is happening (see Chapter 26). Listening more carefully, it wasn't all in Urdu. Perhaps 10% or so were English cricketing terms. I started to list them and within minutes had: batting, batsman, short ball, dot ball, fielder, wicket, catch, white ball wide, sensible batting, long on, leg break, and deep square leg. These and other terms appeared to seamlessly appear within Urdu sentences, although I suspect that, "Bad ball. Very bad ball." may have been switching to English between Urdu sentences.

Then I just let the commentary wash over me, until it returned to English after a few more overs of Urdu. On a 'Don't try this at home.' note, one quickly starts to hear other English words appearing in the foreign commentary. Was that "confidence" that I heard within the Urdu, or just a phoneme string close enough that my mind identified it, with some doubt, as an English word? One view of the human mind is that basically it is a pattern recogniser and it will interpret even genuinely random stimuli as being meaningful; prosaically, seeing pictures in clouds.

Subsequently, I found in my own cricket library that Simon Hughes [3] had provided an example of what I'd been listening to. Here is the young Pakistani Nasir Zaida on the telephone to his parents telling them how he was bowled by a "nasty delivery" from John Emburey, "Nicha vallum balla die punka wallah the ball turned and lifted delli pincha diccum." How trustworthy Simon is on the non-English might be questioned, but what the ball did is pretty clear.

Beyond my own library, Google led me to an excellent article by Nadeem F. Paracha [4]. Apparently, when in 1978 cricket commentary was introduced in Urdu on PTV and Radio Pakistan, at first all the cricket terms were in Urdu. One needs to be bilingual to understand the difficulties, perhaps humorous lapses, of such all Urdu commentary, but clearly the bilingual mixture is now preferred.

A trivial internet search readily informs me that Pakistan has two official languages, Urdu and English. What interests me more is that only 8% of Pakistanis speak Urdu as a first language, but nearly all have it as a second. By circuitous speculation I reach the proposition that a problem for English is that it has native speakers, and wouldn't it be better if "The" global language had no native, first language speakers, but everyone learned it as a second language?

Bill Bryson [1, pp185-6] tells me that more than 50 simplified "universal languages" were invented during the late nineteenth century, but of these only Esperanto survives and even with eight million "claimed" speakers it cannot be judged a success. English is the only realistic candidate for a global language and as such she is used. But how!

But how? Actually really well if the goal is communication. I recently had to read a research paper in an Indian medical journal. I had no problem with the content, but it jarred, it took me longer to read than usual, and by a native English speaker's standards it was illiterate. So? Any reading problems I had were obviously trivial compared to those of the scientists who had to write it in a foreign, second language. Having been an international journal's editor for a dozen years, I am sure that this paper would not get published in the mainstream American and British journals unless all the English were corrected, even though most of the corrections will not change the semantics one jot.

Gideon Haigh [5, p62] provides a similar example

quoting The Indian Premier League's once super mogul, Lalit Modi, verbatim concerning a request for him "to accept the Kochi bid after the official 5pm deadline":

> *I declined to accept the same, saying it was beyond time. You [Manohar] however asked me to accept the bid. You advised me to anti time the bid to 12 noon for 6th March 2010 ... You seemed to be under extreme pressure to ensure that the late bid be included in the bidding process. Since you failed to ensure that the bid be included you then decided to ensure that the bid process itself is cancelled.*

Haigh then concludes, "The wandering tenses were confusing; the inference was clear." While, not withstanding his excellent book, I might dispute that anything about Indian cricket is clear, and I confess that on first reading I didn't notice the "wandering tenses". I might dispute with Gideon his "inference", but Mr. Modi's meaning does seem clear.

There is something wrong, an utter priggishness from native English speakers about the sanctity of their English and it is an Englishman's shame that my own country is in an international vanguard. It is hard to count how many people are native English speakers globally, but an estimated of 300 – 400 million [1, p174] makes the United Kingdom's native speakers a minority, no matter how vociferously is pedants protest. Furthermore, just England is more linguistically diverse than North America or Australia and thus has to resort to a semi-official 'Received Pronunciation', an English dialect few use.

There are no linguistically imperialist nations vying to supplant English as the *de facto* global language, not even the Chinese who, numerically, would have a case for Mandarin. English is already used for the majority of science and engineering publishing, for much international commerce and government, and Pakistan is far from alone in having English as an alternative, second official national language.

The time has come, it should be irresistible, that the world's official language should be Global English (GE). Loosely based on American English on the basis of volume and global reach, in GE definite articles, split infinitives and the numerous other grammatical and stylistic preferences of the native speaking linguistic xenophobes would become optional. The emphasis would be on the minimisation of ambiguity, particularly as ambiguity is disastrous for serious government, commercial, legal, etc. applications where, unlike in science and engineering, mathematics/logic are un-available. The Lalit Modi quote above seems to me to be an example of a perfectly reasonable use of GE and, in such a context, comments about verb wandering are unnecessary. Wandering around some concept of Truth, of course, is another matter.

It should be hoped that GE would never produce Great Literature as, artistically, ambiguity is, perhaps perversely, prized, particularly by the English who, according to an old aphorism of mine, delight in masturbating with their language. They seem to treat it as a competitive hobby and much English humour revolves around deliberate misunderstandings, although mere sexual innuendo is considered low brow.

I won't try to guess how the other English speaking nations will react, but if GE were accepted as the global standard, then that would leave England's linguistic stick-in-the-muds very unhappy. They would be reduced to writing letters to the more serious newspapers complaining of infelicities in what might be called United Kingdom English (UKE). Given the little kingdom's linguistic diversity mentioned above, then the semi-official version might the called Public United Kingdom English, and may it stick in their throats.

Everything I write, of course, is in GE. I simply choose to take the options that makes my GE also that subset which I think of as English English. What I don't do, embarrassed monolingual that I am, is to complain when others make different selections of grammar and style, provided these do not lead to ambiguity. To repeat the last sentence: I am embarrassed monolingual, I don't do complain others choices grammar/style, if not ambiguous.

Accepting GE would not be to agree to linguistic anarchy and 'unique' still wouldn't be allowed to mean 'unknown'. I imagine that if accepted around the world, then GE would evolve by concentrating on the communication of meaning. Global acceptance would remove the brakes of redundant grammar and stylistic conventions propounded, often in great ignorance, by Proper English's public pundits. What would "global acceptance" entail? 'Ay, there's the rub.', which would be a poor sentence in GE because it uses an incomprehensible colloquialism[26].

[1] Bryson, B. (1990) *Mother Tongue: The Story of the English Language*. Penguin.

[2] Booth, L. (2008) *Cricket, Lovely Cricket? An Addict's Guide to the World's Most Exasperating Game.* Yellow Jersey Press.

[3] Hughes, S. (1997) *A Lot of Hard Yakka – Triumph and Torment: A County Cricketer's Life*. Headline.

[4] http://www.dawn.com/news/1128357 - as available on 27/09/2014.

[5] Haigh, G. (2010) *Sphere of Influence: Writings on Cricket and its Discontents*. Simon & Schuster.

---

[26] Shakespeare's "To be …" soliloquy from Hamlet, "To sleep – perchance to dream: ay, there's the rub!" Probably coming from bowls where the 'rub' of the green (grass playing area) is something that causes a bowl to deviate from its course.

Chapter 18

Thank You, Sir Geoffrey.

There may still be a group campaigning for Mr. Geoffrey Boycott, O.B.E. to be knighted, but the continued use of the appellation 'Sir' does reflect public affection for the man in many parts of the cricket playing world[27]. The unimaginative reviewer will be tempted by the phrase 'love him or loathe him' and there are probably around equal numbers in both, large camps.

In the 'loathe him' camp is Dominic Lawson who has published in The Sunday Times' Culture magazine one of the meanest book reviews I've had the misfortune to read [1]. The book reviewed was Boycott's second autobiography, published in 2014, 'Corridor of Certainty' [2]. His first one [3] was published in 1987, which for many people is long ago. I tend to prefer Leo McKinstry's unofficial biography of 2005, 'A Cricketing Hero' [4], because it tries for balance between the love and loathe fanatics. McKinstry's book is clearly very well researched and while, as he says, "this is not, in any sense, an authorized biography", McKinstry thanks Boycott "for his assistance in checking facts and in expediting interviews with several of his friends" (p viii).

Returning to Demonic Lawson, his review gives the impression that Boycott's latest autobiography does not mention cricket at all. Even though the book's subtitle on the slip cover, which Lawson doesn't mention, is 'My Life Beyond Cricket', it is clear from even a cursory glance at

---

[27] The knightly title is usually attributed first to Ron Griffith (1973) "a Barbados-born cricket fanatic" [3, p205; see also 4, p235].

the chapter titles that there is a lot of cricket related material in it. As a rough estimate, only a quarter of the book is about Boycott's cancer rather than about cricket; chapters cancerous are three to five, which is 71 pages out of 265 text pages (71/265 = 26.7%).

Unlike the book, most of the Times' review is about Boycott's cancer and it's treatment, but Lawson manages to top and tail this with mention of the French trial where Boycott was convicted "for violently assaulting a female companion" and that after his cancer diagnosis he "decides to marry 'because if I died I did not want the taxman to get all my money' – how romantic."

My impression from Leo McKinstry is that the French trial and appeal were farcical, which is not to knock England's old enemy as I might at times be equally scathing about the British legal system. Similarly, McKinstry explicitly states, "The timing of their engagement, three months before Boycott even had the first inkling of cancer, contradicts the belief that it was the illness that initially drove him to marriage." [4, p327].

What's so great about romance, Mr. Lawson? Nearly thirty years ago the pregnant, beautiful Japanese girlfriend and I went to a financial advisor to check that we would not be financially worse off if married rather than merely living in sin. I'll admit that I was wrong about marriage, I thought is was just another bit of paper, like the degrees. I used to say that the only advantages to the title doctor were that it made it easier to book restaurant tables, that policemen called you 'Sir', and that it helped filter out junk telephone calls, "There is no Mister Diaper living here." I discovered I was wrong about marriage on the day after our wedding. I woke up next to the person who was now the beautiful Japanese wife and it felt very different from the hundreds of previous mornings waking up beside her. Marriage, I found, is about a lifetime commitment and I'm sure the bJw and I would not have persevered had we remained an unmarried couple.

So, what is so great about romance? Is romance

anything more than a culture's lies, deceptions and delusions that cover what are genuine instincts, sets of genetically programmed, context sensitive, complex behaviours, in this case concerning sexual reproduction (see Chapter 6)? To counter immediate outrage from the romantics, sociobiology is widely accepted by many biological scientists, even though it's application to *Homo Sapiens* remains "controversial".

To commend sociobiology, it is highly interdisciplinary, taking in many areas of scientific psychology, neuroscience and, lots of, biology, e.g. physiology, bio-chemistry and genetics.

To understand sociobiology one has to appreciate its epistemology, which is that branch of philosophy dealing with the nature of knowledge, crudely, what is True. Sociobiology provides an alternative perspective to what most people, historically and now, would consider the common and common sense view. A perspective, or point of view, is a model of the assumed universe created by a set of axioms. Axioms are fundamental statements of belief that cannot be questioned from within the epistemological space they create. Indeed, axioms are notoriously difficult even to identify from within the knowledge space they define.

The basic sociobiological perspective is that what is important biologically is the survival of the genotype and not the phenotype. The human phenotype is the standard issue body of trunk, limbs, head and primary sexual organs. Howsoever we feel about it, sociobiologically the phenotype is unimportant, except as a device to preserve and multiply its genes. Sociobiologically, YOU DON'T MATTER!

It is in a sociobiological context that I question the romance concept. I'm unimpressed with Mr. Lawson's implicit, unquestioning belief that romance is a 'Good Thing'. I think Geoffrey Boycott and I took rational decisions with regard to financing our progeny, attempting to optimise our duty to our genes.

Lawson's main attack is on Boycott's belief's about alternative medicine and similar exotica. On Test Match Special I've heard Sir Geoffrey wax on his oriental and similar beliefs. From any post-Enlightenment, rational, and particularly scientific, perspective, I'm afraid Boycott's beliefs are rubbish, or "roobish" if Lawson has got the Yorkshire accent correct.

To clarify my 'rubbish', but to cut out a great deal of philosophy, history and so on, our modern world is built on the development of scientific knowledge starting from some three hundred years ago. Alternative or folk medicines can culturally evolve to sometimes provide effective remedies, but their associated belief systems, why a medicine works, are just nowhere near as good as our science ones. Technically, in comparison to science, their 'predictive adequacy' is poor.

Are Lawson's own beliefs any less rubbish than Sir Geoffrey's? I think not. After all, Lawson starts his review by introducing himself as in 1998 being "the editor of The Sunday Telegraph". I can think of two good things to say about the Telegraph newspapers of that era. First, they had an excellent, traditional cryptic crossword. Second, metaphorically they were printed in blue ink and their right wing bias to news reports was relatively easy to remove[28]. One must surely have some very odd beliefs to edit a newspaper that is so proudly conservative and Conservative, and perhaps even stranger ones to publicly admit, willingly, to doing it.

When I'm dismissive of people's beliefs, the beautiful Japanese wife calls me "arrogant". I protest. Arrogance is like thinking you are at the top of a mountain looking down, pejoratively, on those below. In contrast, I am at

---

[28] The problem with most of the serious British liberal, with a small 'l', leaning newspapers is that political bias varies with different reporters so it is far more difficult to try and eliminate such bias than when one can be sure that all the reporters are someway right of some notional political centre ground.

the bottom of a deep well. I don't believe in anything. Technically, I write of the *assumed* universe and that everything is just models, of models, of models. I choose to use different axioms, different perspectives and, therefore, different models in differing situations and in my research work and daily life, for anything serious, I will use several different models and more than one axiomatically different perspective.

It's not comfortable at the bottom of my well where above me resides nearly everyone else, believing this or that, whether it's all due to fairies at the bottom of the garden, astrology, astronomy, archaeology or whatever the ex-editor of The Sunday Telegraph bizarrely believes. Properly, I reserve my criticisms to the consequences of people's beliefs. I suppose I must forgive Lawson as I do Boycott for what they believe, but as both are public figures, I wonder, with their different beliefs, who has done more damage, or good, to other people?

Geoffrey Boycott is not a genius. Nor is he well educated. I recall a definition from when I was a teenager that defined a genius as someone who excelled in more than one, radically different, area of human endeavour[29]. The example was Albert Einstein who apart from the science was also a concert level violinist. Geoffrey Boycott is the opposite of a genius, he is a super specialist. That's why it's easy for me to smile and just ignore his non-cricketing beliefs.

Boycott is a super specialist on cricket. There is nothing to be ashamed of in being self taught. Indeed, at the very highest levels it is inevitable as only the expert can teach the expert. I observe, however, that one way to recognise the real McCoy expert from the charlatan, the second rater or worse, is that experts are always prepared to learn. Desperate to learn because to be the best of the

---

[29] This definition only works after the knowledge explosion of the 20th. Century whereas someone a hundred years or more earlier could master nearly all human knowledge.

best, then someone must have devoted all, or nearly all, of their life to acquiring their expertise. With age comes the wisdom and hence humility that there is always more to learn, which is not to say that super experts find it easy to suffer fools gladly. I have a foot in the pro-Boycott camp because I recognise a fellow monomaniac's devotion to their life's work.

McKinstry notes that "Boycott is often dismissed as a monomaniac" [4, p219], and continues, "and certainly this might have been true in his early days when he lived only for cricket", before detailing Boycott developing wider interests. Far from dismissing monomania, I'm all for it in professionals who are super experts in their complicated area of endeavour.

Without any criticism of any of the regular live commentators on TMS or BBC local radio, Geoffrey Boycott is the best. My personal experience of Geoffrey is only via his radio commentaries. As a player I know of him only from the radio, quite a lot over the years from this about his playing cricket, and from books. Boycott must feature in cricket books nearly as commonly as W.G. and Bradman. These players appear not only in the cricket histories, but in most humorous and anecdotal cricket books as well. It's not whether this triumvirate do appear in a cricket book, but what sort of book about cricket doesn't mention Grace and Bradman, and following behind them, Boycott? It's not essential to mention them, but is at least common[30].

---

[30] Other people are welcome to do more detailed research, but to quickly check my hypothesis about Grace, Bradman and Boycott, I looked at the index of 'Cricket: A Very Peculiar History'[5], which I was re-reading at the time, and counted named players' index entries. The index (pp188-192) is quite good for a little, funny book. Top scoring with six index entries were Grace, Bradman and Sachin Tendulkar, with runners up with five citations being Boycott, Shane Warne and Brian Lara. Best of the rest were Ian Botham and Viv Richards with four entries apiece.

My rehearsed description of why I rate so highly Sir Geoffrey The Commentator goes, "Live, immediately after a ball is bowled, Boycott is able to give an accurate description of the ball bowled, which he does on anything near being an interesting ball. You can check on the slow motion replays and he is nearly always right: it was straying down leg side; there was an inside edge; it did pitch outside the line of leg stump; it didn't carry; and on and accurately on."

I can elaborate, that I think Geoffrey is so good because of the way he treated batting, how he learned, what he did, his attitude to batting. His regularly repeated aphorisms, "You can't make runs back in the pavilion." being but one favourite, makes his attitude clear now. So well known is he that if someone referred to 'a Boycottian innings', few might quibble with a definition of as 'a slow century'.

I am not alone in my views. Leo McKinstry [4, p270] quotes "Bill Sinrich, the senior vice-president of TransWorld" concerning the 1990 Caribbean tour and Boycott:

> "*If you blindfolded Geoffrey after something happened at real speed, and then you asked him to narrate the replay in slow motion, without seeing the screen, he could do it. The incident will have formed an image in his mind so precise and immediate, he does not need to look at the replay. That is a unique skill.*"

Yes, to all that, except that it is not a unique skill (Chapter 17). I rate David Townsend (DT) very highly in the same commentator's role.

Additionally, Mr. Sinrich praises Geoffrey's rapid adoption of the emerging television cricket technologies. If you are a super expert at something, then adapting it with equal thoroughness, again, thank you Mr. Sinrich, to a different aspect of the same thing is what I expect. It's not genius, but taking a vast, expert store of specialised knowledge and using it in a different way; it's just another aspect of an insatiable desire to learn more.

'Boycottian', or similar, does have other definitions, such as mentioning uncovered wickets, as in, "Uncovered wickets, that was a very Boycottian thing to say." That Jonathan (Aggers) Agnew is a stirrer in the Brian Johnston tradition and relentlessly eggs Poor Sir Geoffrey on, but makes for cricket commentary of today as good, if not better, than in decades gone by. Watching cricket on the radio, my 'Gold Standard' is Test Match Special. Thank you one and all, and, thank you, Sir Geoffrey.

[1] Lawson, D. (2014) *'Memoirs' review of Corridor of Certainty.* The Sunday Times Culture magazine, 44-45. 14/09/2014.

[2] Boycott, G. (2014) *Corridor of Certainty: My Life Beyond Cricket.* Simon & Schuster.

[3] Boycott, G. (1987) *Boycott: The Autobiography.* Macmillan.

[4] McKinstry, L. (2005) *Geoff Boycott: A Cricketing Hero.* HarperSport: HarperCollins.

[5] Pipe, J. (2012) *Cricket: A Very Peculiar History with Added Googlies.* Book House, Salariya Book Company.[31]

[31] Although this book is a couple or so years old, I'd recommend it as a Christmas present for either: (1) a moderate cricket 'follower' who might find it suitable for Boxing Day or when sitting contemplating leg theory in 'the smallest room'; or, (2) for a youth, a prepubescent person, and abjuring sexism, put it in her or his Christmas stocking; it's better than a plastic pink equine with combable mane. Of necessity, given its length, the book's a bit didactic, but overall fair fun.

Chapter 19

Padding Down.

According to an American, military technology focused programme that I caught a while ago on television, these days the latest body armour is light weight, thin and flexible but will protect its wearer from most small arms fire, even at point blank range. Unlike bullets, a sphere is the least penetrative of projectile shapes and cricket balls travel an order of magnitude (ten times) more slowly than bullets. In the future, could we make cricket clothes of such military grade stuff?

I imagine making something like an armoured wetsuit, in white for test cricket. Against such an idea is the aesthetics of cricketers prancing around looking like fancy dress victims at an American comic book superheroes convention. These protective suits could be worn as long johns under conventional cricket clothes, but to what point? The new suits will be thermally efficient, allow perspiration out appropriately, etc., so any outer clothes would only be cosmetic and potentially disadvantageous. Most disadvantageous for batsmen as ball or bat catching clothes can, and sometimes does, deceive umpires that contact was bat and ball and out.

No more would batsmen, wicket keepers or short fielders need pads. It would certainly be easier running between the wickets unencumbered by the big, clunky pads of today. No pads but no pain would, however, seriously affect how batsmen play. Apart from not having to avoid bouncers, the gate, the space between bat and pads, would be considerably larger and this would make defence harder notwithstanding the current leg before wicket laws. As a design issue, batsmen might want to wear pads to protect their wicket and not their legs, the latter being adequately catered for by the new suits. This is how I got to a more serious issue than speculating about full body armour cricket clothing.

With such modern military materials it must already be possible to redesign batsmen's pads so that they are lighter and, critically, smaller than those currently used. Basically, now, money no object, a batsman could have any shape of pad they liked. Whatever the shape, the degree of protection of the covered parts would be the same. So what shape to choose?

Design step back: what are the functions of a batsman's pads, apart from protecting shins and knees from bowled ball injury? Do they protect from other causes of injury? For example, when sliding "full length" to make ones ground running a dodgy one? Probably not as most of such sliding is on the torso.

Design is pretty well always about compromise, so a dirty design concept is negative functionality, what a design prevents one doing[32]. Thus batsman's pads made of reinforced concrete would provide an excellent solution to the primary functionality of leg protection, but at the unacceptable expense of being too heavy for batsmen to move, making being "stuck in the crease" literal. Generally, functionality (what something does, or, at least, is supposed to do) is expressed positively, so, apart from their primary protective function, batsmen's pads should also facilitate playing around the crease and running between the wickets.

What makes design fun is that it is creative. I think the

---

[32] There are many cases where design does deliberately prevent people doing some things, most obviously in safety critical situations (there really are some combinations of things one never wants to do in an aeroplane or in a dangerous industrial plant, chemical or nuclear for example). In software engineering a major problem for designers of business systems is that users will take short cuts to save themselves time but at the cost to their organisation of possible data integrity and security failures.

following question is an example: '*What does the batsman generally want to happen to a ball after it hit his pads*?' Who has asked this question before and particularly, were any of them involved in pad design and what did they do about it?

To address the main question, a crude categorisation as a starter might be three fold. After hitting a batsman's pads the ball might: (1) drop to ground and stop or trickle away safely; (2) leave at speed off the ground to allow safe leg byes or bat-pad runs; or (3) pop into the air, with or without groundspeed (great vertical velocity rarely being a desideratum). Obviously the last is least desirable as bat-pad-catches are likely. The first is the safest option for a batsman. As for the second, I question how desperate are batsmen for leg byes and, I hope more importantly, that I'm in an informed majority who believe that batting is principally about scoring runs from the bat.

On such categorisation and analysis I can now consider pad designs that might support the additional functional requirement that after a ball hits the pads it should drop to ground with minimum velocity. Note, it is "pad designs" plural as what I've called 'Diaper's Gulf' in my engineering writing is the gap between requirements and design, which must involve creativity as it cannot be bridged by formal methods (mathematics/logic) or too rigidly designed procedures.

An early design I tried was to have pads with horizontal, triangular, downward facing slats which would force the ball towards the ground. Against this are what happens when the ball hits the leading edge of the triangular slats. Even worse, one cannot assume that the batsmen's lower leg will be near vertical with the ground at contact.

A much better design would be to go for maximum energy absorption by the pad, leaving the ball with no kinetic energy and so only being able to drop by gravity to the ground. Easy! The outside of the pad is covered by one or more soft plastic cells filled with a gel. Some laboratory research would need to determine optimal, three dimensional cell size, gel viscosity and related properties.

An additional refinement would be to make the outside of the pad slightly sticky which would allow more time for energy to be drained from the ball while in contact with the pad. One couldn't use a glue if this could be transferred to the ball, which would be a new form of ball tampering, akin to Lillie's aluminium bat damaging the ball (see Chapter 2). Fortunately, there is a "science of interacting surfaces in relative motion" [33] which is tribology and I'd have to leave it to such experts to develop some none ball damaging pad surface that briefly grips the ball.

Cricket's a game so The Authorities could simply legislate against the above, gel cells and sticky surfaces. Unfortunately, *le mot just* would be "simply" legislate on past evidence. Furthermore, once the idea's public then what is to stop minor redesign of batsmen's current pads so that their outer surface is softer, stickier and so more energy absorbing? The self confessed cricket addict Alex Britten [1] reviews the development of batsmen's pads, noting that there has been little visible change in a century although modern "ultra-light materials such as PVC" are now used. He also illustrates the smooth Aero pads which were unsegmented and more the sort of design I might have in mind.

Alex says that, "The biggest modification of cricket pad design has been the move from buckle straps to velcro, so I fear there will not be any major development in pad fashion in the near future." Awash with television money, I'm not so sure he is right. I am sure that there are large numbers of cricket traditionalists who are utterly delighted at the lack of development; some are still around from when they complained about Packer's pyjama cricket circus.[34]

---

[33] Concise Oxford English Dictionary, 7th. Ed.

[34] I try very hard to never imagine what MCC members wear in bed.

What worries me more is the effect a completely successful redesign of batsmen's pads would have on cricket. It could be profound and, I worry, not at all a Good Thing for the game. The new pad technology is perfect, let us imagine; if the ball hits the pads it will fall to the ground at the batsman's feet. So with spin bowlers there will be less reason for forward short and silly fielding, the ball will not carry from bat to pad to fielder, not even if they are Brian Close close to the bat. To faster bowlers the slips will just have to stay back for an outside edge, it will never carry off the new pads, but caught edges are more common at slip than bat-pad catches. On a more positive note, perhaps medium or fast bowlers could overcome the new pads to the extent that forward silly/short fielders could act as they do currently for spinners. The point here is that just changing pad design could significantly affect fielding positions and hence both tactics and strategy. I'm sure cricket would survive such changes, but remembering Bobby Simpson's view that cricket is a great game, but played by idiots (see Chapter 7), I wonder how long it would take cricket professionals, players and analysts, to adapt.

This chapter started from idle speculation of a futuristic fantasy involving adapting state-of-the-art military personnel body armour for cricket players. Some categorisation and analysis identified a secondary functional requirement that after striking the pad the ball should drop to the ground with minimum velocity. A kinetic energy absorbing design illustrates that this requirement could be achieved with some degree of success, if not fully. It is suggested that pad redesign could significantly affect how cricket is played, for example, by changing traditional fielding positions. Such engineering might therefore be considered rather more than mere "fashion" as suggested by Britten.

There are other issues about pad design that could be addressed, for example, pad shape given that military grade materials could make pads much thinner than those currently used, which howsoever modern don't use military technology.

Other equipment, not only for batsmen but also for wicket keepers and short fielders, could also be redesigned using the latest materials. Body padding and arm guards, obviously, but also headgear ('helmet' might not be the future accurate term as it implies a class of design solution) and, probably most difficult of all, gloves. With international cricket so wealthy, then expense in this specialist market is far less important than performance. No doubt materials technology will continue to improve and so the design of top end cricket equipment will become more driven by analysing requirements and less by the host of materials available or possible to engineer.

I have qualms about all these sort of changes and I can even agree with some of the arguments of those who are passionately agin it all. They nor I, however, will stop cricket developing. My crystal ball may be cracked but I can see futures coming through the glass darkly. My primary message is to those who administer cricket, to rise from their slumbers and start to prepare. The authorities reacted to aluminium bats by banning all substances for these not made of wood. This won't work with modern materials, which like synthetic illegal drugs, will remain steps ahead of any banning authority. The options are either a do nothing *laissez faire* or effect some sophisticated control. For example, to counter the proposed increased stickiness of batsman's pads, some measure like a maximum coefficient of friction could be specified. I fear that the authorities, ICC out of MCC, will be traditional and fall between these two options, being tardily reactive and not taking a well prepared proactive role.

PostScript

Two days after I finished the first draft of this chapter, the 10th. November, 2014, I was watching the Pakistan v. New

Zealand 1st. Test, day two, session one. At just after 6:30am GMT the television commentator, I think it was Ramiz Raja, said that there was a lot of technology being put into batsmen's pad and glove design so that they would prevent "rebound". He continued, that this could "take out short fielders." Good. Not one iota of my pleasure at doing the concept level design decreased because others are thinking along the same lines. Indeed, I consider it complimentary that professionals are confirming my, mere enthusiast's, ideas.

Coincidence, synchronicity (Chapter 9) or as I suspect, that such pairs of events, as we perceive them, are far more probable than we tend to believe. I'd been thinking about this chapter for about a quarter of a year, therefore I would have been primed to be alerted to the topic of pad design, one of many for this book, so I guess I hadn't heard comments about these professional developments over this three month period.

Positively, the professional work reinforces my conclusion that ICC *et al.* should be anticipating technical developments in cricket kit.

[1] Britten, A. (2013) *Thoughts of a Cricket Addict: Changing Cricket Fashion – The Pads.* https://alexbritten.wordpress.com/2013/01/22/changing-cricket-fashion-the-pads/ (accessed 07/11/2014).

Chapter 20

Better BBC Cricket – for FREE!

While I've followed England Test cricket for a quarter century or so, I only discovered recently the County games through the BBC local radio's commentaries. I think my first full season was 2012, three seasons before drafting this chapter.

By the end of the 2014 season I had reached the point where given the option of a four day County Championship match on the radio versus a one day England match streamed to the television and coupled with the Test Match Special radio commentary, then I was choosing the former. This was a rational decision involving quite a few, competing criteria. Least important to me is whether there is a live video stream available and close to the bottom of my criteria list is England's performance, which in ODIs against India was woeful in 2014, although England did win the one and only Twenty20 match against India.

At the other end of my scale there is simply my strong preference for red ball cricket, itself a complex, rational decision, and between are criteria to do with TMS versus BBC local radio commentary, the potential for interactivity with the commentators, scheduling of play and intervals, and so on.

While varying in style, in terms of technical cricket commentary, all the BBC local radio matches that I've sampled have been uniformly good. Furthermore, they have a charm now diminished from TMS which these days is perhaps over resourced, has too many commentators, although it would be invidious to choose between them as all are very good, and TMS is slickly produced, in contrast to its struggles of yesteryear (see Peter Baxter's books [1, 2] or many others produced by the TMS team, for example [3, 4, 5, 6]).

It is very obvious that BBC local radio cricket commentary is not over resourced. Sometimes there are just two commentators, which must be hard work over four days, although the fifty over matches take even a little longer in a day (100 v. 96 overs), and have only a single interval. Of course there is room for improvement. How could it be otherwise with something as complicated as cricket? Indeed, it would probably be relatively easy to be peevish and produce a wish list as long as the proverbial arm. With limited, stretched resources, however, the critical criterion for wish list winnowing is that any suggestions for improvements are free.

From my user's point of view, BBC cricket services can be divided in two: (1) the BBC web pages; and (2) the live radio commentaries. While this chapter concludes with a few comments on the latter, it is the web pages, which includes the live scorecard, which is the main focus of this chapter. This is so because the BBC's cricket web pages are more complex than most, primarily because they are dynamic, and so they must be resource hungry, also known as 'expensive'. Without going into economics and accountancy, it is easier to suggest improvements to expensive things which don't materially add to current costs, i.e. improvements for free.

I'd love to visit a BBC centre, hub, facility, or whatever they call it in BBC management speak, where the cricket web pages are prepared and updated. Admittedly this may not be most people's beverage of choice, but I've visited numerous organisation of many types during my working life. I was, and probably still am, an internationally recognised expert in what is called 'Task Analysis' (TA). Really, I'm not keen on writing what appears as chest-thumping boastfulness, but I've published books and many research papers on TA. For independent, numerical evidence one can try my 'Google Test of Fame'. Insert someone's name, for example "Dan Diaper", into Google, or other search engine of your choice, and look at the thousands of hits and for how many tens, hundreds or thousands of pages they extend to. Particularly important if one uses my name is that you include the double quotes as otherwise you will get a lot of miss-hits to do with things to put on babies' bottoms. Anyway, going into an organisation and studying what it does has been at the core of my scientific and research engineering career, which is why I would like to visit a BBC website centre.

A second reason why I'd like to visit the BBC is because I was researching hypertext before the World Wide Web was invented by Tim Berners Lee in 1990. Hypertext is the technology on which all web pages are based. One can still see this in web page addresses and file extensions such as .html, which stands for HyperText Mark-up Language. I am genuinely interested in the IT involved, and, of course, the people involved.

I may just be an old cynic, but I do wonder if BBC local radio hasn't inherited legacy servers to host their web pages. These, I imagine, having been passed down from more prestigious and/or deemed more important parts of the BBC. I may be wrong and BBC local radio may have the very latest kit, but on a typical day I will lose the BBC radio commentary half a dozen times. Moreover, it happens on all my machines, the hardwired tower PC and, via my home wifi, my LifeBook and brand new laptop. Whether I can be considered fortunate or not may be moot, but I missed the whole of Middlesex's first match of the 2014 season at Hove, a humiliating defeat for Middlesex, because the commentary dropped out every couple of minutes. Sometimes the foreign servers, for example in India, which I use to stream live television are more reliable than the BBC local radio stream. I have been reduced, admittedly only occasionally and reluctantly, to having to abandon BBC radio and watch with the television commentary on. Overall, I think the BBC local radio commentary service was more reliable in 2014 than in previous years, or I may just have become more tolerant. In any case, this is an irrelevant whinge because servers are expensive and I'm looking for ways to improve the BBC cricket services for free.

As an IT professional, I'm not sure if I suffer more or less than less IT qualified users. I am highly sensitive to errors, of both content and of design. Professionally I am sympathetic to the BBC's difficulties that arise from updating their main cricket website several times a day, and updating some subsidiary pages more often, and each score card every two minutes.

I'm not really bothered by typographic errors, they are bound to occur with free text entry and even when they involve data such as a score, date or day of play, these can usually be found correctly on other pages, such as the scorecard. To give the BBC a plus, broken hypertext links are surprisingly infrequent; I can think of only a couple of occurrences in 2014 and I obtained access by going to other BBC pages.

First on the negative side, however, please get the start of transmission times right. At present (2014), the BBC design for County matches is to simply list the start of play, as is listed in the match schedules. Commentary has got to start, at least I think, a few minutes before the first ball is bowled and I don't see why on the radio options pages the transmission start time is not provided. What would it cost (irony)?

Similarly, during an unscheduled break in play, frequent in rainy Britain, why not give out the time play is expected to be resumed on the website, just as start times or an 'in-play' message is displayed. Even better, report when the next umpires' pitch inspection is due. I assume that this information is readily available from the live radio commentators who, even if off-air, must still be monitoring the day. The place to put this is on the match schedules as I will skip to other matches if the one I've chosen to follow is significantly affected by rain (or other causes of delay). On some days I've switched to three or four different games following the better weather around the country. Making my choices would be much easier if I could reliably see the state of play, expected times of pitch inspections or resumptions of play, on one web page so that I can more sensibly plan where on local radio I am to go, and when.

In the days, long ago, when I only had radio, then I used a cribbage board to record the overs bowled during a day's play (see Chapter 4). Now I use the BBC's match score card from their website, which is updated every two minutes. I use this very frequently as it contains the basic numbers that I need to calculate how the match is progressing.

The two minute update time isn't a problem, it's only about half an over, and I've got the live BBC local radio commentary for what is happening on the field. What is a problem is that on each refresh the score card returns to the top of its window. Thus, excepting for the opening batsmen in the match's first inning, one loses the part of the scorecard that one is looking at every two minutes. This is very silly, very annoying, and very completely unnecessary. It's a standard feature on many interactive websites that after an update the web page returns to where the user was last looking. There must be many little Java apps that can do this, even if it isn't a standard feature of the BBC's website software.

What I have to do is to carefully place my mouse cursor on the top-of-the-page text hyperlink that will relocate me to the innings' details I'm studying. Then when a refresh occurs, I can do a single mouse click to get back to where I want to be, provided I don't move the mouse. This is called a "workaround". What it shows is that I have a functional requirement, to keep viewing the same part of a webpage after a refresh occurs. I resent having to resort to such clumsy, manual methods for the BBC's want of a trivial bit of software.

Still on the BBC's scorecard, at the bottom are listed the players and umpires' names. It is useful to give players' full names as commentators often refer to them by either first or surname. We only get the umpires' initials with their family name, which might hark back to the, now thankfully abandoned, social distinctions in naming between amateurs and professionals. Usefully, the captain and wicket keeper are designated by either (C) or (W) following their name. What I would like is more of this.

I have much railed, Chapter 6 being devoted to it, that radio cricket commentators repeatedly fail to remind me whether a batsman is right or left handed. I cannot properly watch cricket on the radio without this essential information. If only the BBC could indicate each batsman's handedness after their name, then this would solve the problem for me and anyone else who has the radio commentary and full scorecard available simultaneously. It would cost nothing to add this information in the same way as the captain and wicket keeper are identified, just an (R) or (L) after each player's name, or symbols could be used, e.g. < and > for right and left handers, respectively[35]. Please?

While less essential, I'd be happy with other post nominal information about each player after their name on the team list. Whether bowlers are left or right handed would be good, and what about adding something about their speed. On the latter, I'd start with F, M or S, for 'Fast', 'Medium' or 'Slow/Spin' and so avoid endless discussion on the differences between "medium fast" and "fast medium" bowling (on grammatical grounds I think medium fast is the faster). All this sort of information is readily available within the BBC, from the radio commentators if no one else, and the few additional keystrokes to player's names is cost free.

---

[35] I quite fancy these text symbols as being in the grandest old traditions of cricket. A left pointing symbol '<' indicates a right handed batsman. It seems obvious to me, looking at it from the bowler's end, but really it needs a bit more consideration of the ergonomic design.

Technically, from a general systems perspective (see Chapter 13), all organisational changes do cost something, if only in the start-up change management, but such costs associated with what I propose above are utterly trivial given the overall cost of the BBC's County cricket coverage. Please, at least start by listing batsmen's handedness.

Turning to the BBC's live cricket commentaries, partly by design and partly due to the weather, and a little partly to do with the reliability of the BBC's servers, in the first half of 2014 I followed many different County matches at many different grounds. Apart from the batsman's handedness issue, all the commentaries were technically excellent at describing the cricket, more than good enough for me to watch on the radio. I did find considerable differences in style, most noticeably what was "discussed" around the cricket (see Chapter 15 for examples), but also differences in the manner that the available technology was used.

Never being a fan but being a follower of Good Cricket (Chapter 10), I found that I could have both Good Commentary and Good Cricket. For the second half of the 2014 County season I settled down and, when they were playing, followed Durham. I did so because of the commentary and I commend to all live radio commentators the Martin Emmerson Model for Excellent Cricket Commentary (MEMECC).

Below I identify four technical aspects of MEMECC which it would cost nothing for all other cricket commentators to adopt. My examples are not intended to be exhaustive, but if they just stimulate some thought and discussion amongst the commentary experts then I'd be satisfied. For me, Durham won the Live Cricket Commentary Championship in 2014. I hope this is the gauntlet other BBC local radio commentators will pick up.

The first of my MEMECC items is easy: start early! At the beginning of every session, do not wait until the first ball is about to be bowled before going on-air. There's always a useful summary to do and the fielding positions need describing, I'd prefer *must* be described, before the first ball. It seems so obvious that it seems silly to write it, but I noticed this problem quite frequently in 2014.

Second, leave the external microphone on in the intervals, all of them, lunch, tea and unscheduled ones. I like this because it makes me feel at the ground, the susurration of the crowd is enough, but I also appreciate the announcements from the ground's loudspeakers; these can be particularly informative during rain intervals when the radio commentators are off air[36]. On a mundane technical note, it reassures me that the BBC's server is still running.

Third, read emails and tweets promptly and regularly. Martin is way, way ahead of the field on this. He reads all of them, in full, usually well within twenty minutes of sending when he is on-air. Many times I've heard apologies from commentators that they are "behind with" or "have forgotten" emails and tweets. It seems half of them can't or won't access email, although I find the emails generally better and more interesting than many tweets, which too often are bare fan slogans. I confess I'm not a tweeterer, but I have learned about sending emails to commentators and I put considerable effort into the ones I send.

My view is that communications from the radio audience should help the commentators and particularly so during slow passages of play and when a match is "petering out" to "an inevitable draw." Often the live commentators are multitasking so it behoves emailers to be helpful and sensible, which will also increase the

---

[36] TMS, of course, is excellently excellent during all the intervals and I've been delighted to have them in my home for hours at a time discussing, mostly, things cricket related. Sometimes it's like a live audio book. Without TMS's resources, I think BBC local radio commentators deserve their lunch and tea, they often put in long, uninterrupted hours of commentary during play.

chances of their message being read out. Obviously, keep it brief, use short sentences, have an interesting point and if you can manage it, a soupson of humour (the threshold is pretty low) no doubt helps. My success at getting emails read out certainly improved over the first half of the 2014 season as I refined my style. I was fortunate to be dubbed "Dr. Dan' early on, but other regulars are also given monikers in what should be jolly chit-chat.

Fourth and finally, like Boy Scouts, commentators should 'be prepared'. They need a computer that works and which they know how to work. I could certainly do with less on-air discussion of how to log on to the cloud, what are the necessary registrations and passwords, etc. Marvellous Martin keeps a dongle in his kitbag, so he can get internet access where all around him his colleagues fail. He also has his own light meter which he sometimes hangs out of the commentary box window. After one long geographical discussion I suggested he should add a compass to his kit as well.

I realise that this chapter may be a hostage to fortune and that by the time the book is published that many of my suggestions will have been adopted independently. Excellent if that were so, the sooner the better and the sooner I'll be even happier. My only use of the BBC's services is to follow cricket. I reckon I get good value for my licence fee already, but there is always room for improvement, particularly if it can be done on a budget, or better, basically for free.

[1] Baxter, P. (2010) *Inside the Box: My Life with Test Match Special*. Aurum.

[2] Baxter, P. (2013) *Can Anyone Hear Me? Testing Times with Test Match Special on Tour*. Corinthian Books.

[3] Martin-Jenkins, C. (2012) *CMJ: A Cricketing Life*. Simon & Schuster.

[4] Frindall, B. (2006) *Bearders: My Life in Cricket.* Orion.

[5] Agnew, J. (2010) *Thanks, Johnners: An Affectionate Tribute to a Broadcasting Legend.* HarperCollins.

[6] Blofeld, H. (2000) *A Thirst for Life with the Accent on Cricket.* Hodder and Stoughton.

Chapter 21

Captaincy's Dark Arts.

If Mike Brearley is so intelligent, why is he a psychoanalyst? Other than the 'psycho' prefix relating to the study of mind, the psycho*analytical* and the psycho*logical* approaches have little in common. There is no scientific evidence for the theoretical basis of psychoanalysis and there cannot be because it is not based on a scientific theory or approach. The existence of Freud's basic theoretical concepts, the id, ego and superego, are unsupported fantasy, fairies at the bottom of the garden.

This is not to deny that psychoanalysis can help people. The basic, cynical, American parody is that, of course, if you have a wise, apparently, and sympathetic listener who will allow you to self indulgently talk about yourself for hours, and *to whom you pay a lot of money*, then of course you, the patient, client, payee, will believe it does you good; and it may. In terms of experimental social psychology, one is in the domain of Cognitive Dissonance Theory [1] and post-choice bias.

It is a large and highly reliable[37], experimental social psychological phenomenon, that after choosing one of two things that were initially judged as equally desirable, then, post choice, the one selected is rated more highly than the one rejected. The *post hoc* (after the event) rationale is pretty simple, "If I chose this one, then it must be better than the other one." The effect is greater when the

---

[37] Reliable in that one can guarantee that undergraduate experiments on this will "work"; perhaps the hardest of all criteria to fulfil.

rewards or the costs are greater. Thus, investing money, time and personal resources ("I could only tell it to my shrink."), it must be expected that people, of a suitable disposition, will benefit from psychoanalysis. The psychoanalytical procedures, so much loved by legions of cartoonists, can work even though the theories are utter bunk.

I am going to write many good things about Mike Brearley's "Art of Captaincy" [2], first published in 1985, but if you have the later edition (2001), as I do, then I can't really recommend its new introduction 'In retrospect, 2001' (pp1-9). Of course I would never recommend that things should be unread, but be warned.

What worries me is that this introduction revolves around psychoanalytical concepts like anxiety. It sounds plausible, such as (pp5-6) "... it is up to the captain, and coach, to help players with self-defeating attitudes that arise individually or collectively as a result of their anxieties." First, could such attitudes arise from mental things other than anxiety? What about, to suggest a few of many, causes such as envy, detestation of one or more fellow players, selfishness, conformity to social norms, or lack of confidence? Any of these could be substituted for "anxieties" in the quote and made to sound equally plausible. I fear the typical psychoanalytical reply is to recast such alternatives in terms of their preferred terminology, so, for example, 'lack of confidence' causes anxiety or, even, that confidence is just the opposite pole of a dimension of anxiety. This leads to the second, more serious problem, how to define anxiety.

I am indebted to Dr. Mike Sheldon, who was often my tutor during my first degree [38], who taught me, in a different context, that in science the name of a thing should be irrelevant and that a simple test is to replace such with 'X' and see what remains. The point is that

---

[38] B.Sc. Psychology, University of Newcastle-upon-Tyne, 1973-6.

psychoanalytical concepts like anxiety, to a considerable extent, rely on a popular, cultural, often implicit, understanding of such concepts. This is 'folk' psychology and against it is that virtually no progress was made in the 'philosophy of mind', as it was once called, for several millennia, until after the first scientific psychology laboratories were established in the 1880s, at Cambridge and Leipzig universities. At least in physics some basics have become folk knowledge, that the Earth orbits its sun or that stuff is made of atoms, but today's folk psychology remains in a medieval, pre-scientific state. I don't trust any of it.

I have little knowledge of how Mike Brearley was unfortunately washed up on the shifty shores of psychoanalysis. I was lucky in that being a teenage, gifted biologist, I studied psychology as "The Science of the Mind" from the off. Chance, opportunity, someone or two he met, where he worked outside of cricket, Mike chose psychoanalysis rather than psychology. These things happen. We were all young and foolish once. I only wish Mike Brearley, arguably the greatest international cricket captain ever, not just of England, will embrace a more sophisticated, scientifically reliable psychology in our dotage.

I was delighted to hear Mike on the radio in 2014, I assume it was on TMS. I recognised that voice. I have heard it from some psychologist colleagues; it is slow, calm, reassuring, reasonable, honest, trustworthy, interested, supportive, and worth a fortune in private practice. I can, well enough, do it, but Mike's an expert. As I'd expect, what he said in the commentary box was extremely sensible, but with the honeyed syrup in his voice you could, I imagine, almost believe it if he said that a half volley outside leg stump to a seven–two offside field was an ideal delivery[39].

---

[39] Interesting pub cricket game? Theoretically, what is the worst possible ball to bowl?

Have any cricket professionals got a bad word to say about Mike Brearley? Even the greatest have been open to criticism: W.G. is widely lambasted for his sharp practices on and off field; The Don was not universally popular in the dressing room and his influence on Australian administration has been questioned. Simon Hughes [3] provides an excellent example eulogy in his section called 'The Conjuror's Final Act' (pp91-95) which starts by saying of Brearley, "He was a brilliant leader with great vision", before providing some examples. Do be careful, however, of the Richie Benaud and Hughes' concept of luck. It is probably due to how people misperceive the probability of things, so one can make one's luck or, as an alternative explanation, be open to creating and exploiting opportunities that occur more frequently than people expect.

Nor is it only the pros. At the amateur end of cricket the pro-Brearley adulation of his captaincy is equally rife. Michael Simkins [4], for example, starts his 'Wokingham' chapter (p181) thus, "In his masterwork, *The Art of Captaincy*, Mike Brearley, … generally considered to be the keenest brain ever to turn his hand to the summer game".

With my metaphorical microscope I have found a fly in the Brearley ointment. In their pornographically subtitled book, Roger Morgan-Grenville and Richard Perkins [5] report (p100) "acquiring a discounted copy of Mike Brearley's The Art of Captaincy …(which) surely had a thing or two to offer us. Not, necessarily, as it turned out." Their basic point is that, "Clearly much of what he writes is not applicable to a club like ours … so we developed our own take on his headings." As to their final comment on their copy's destination, "Many years later, Mike Breaerley's book is propping up a work-bench in my potting shed" (p115), in contrast, my copy resides in the 'Serious–Theory' section of my cricket library, on a shelf above and at the opposite end to where I locate Morgan-Grenville and Perkins (in 'Humour–Team–Duffers').

No matter how modest might be one's cricket library, Brearley's 'The Art of Captaincy' should be one of the half dozen essential books to own, read and, hopefully, re-read. While Morgan-Grenville and Perkins' main aim is humour, at which they do a jolly good job, they miss what is important in Brearley by baulking at his examples as being inappropriate to their team's circumstances. The important stuff, which is very obvious to me, is about acquiring more sophisticated views of people, as individuals and as social organisms in groups and within organisations. Once one has some understanding of this stuff, then Mike's examples can be appropriately adapted. That Mike Brearely has to belabour what is obvious to me reflects that we both do see the world differently from most other people.

Whatever my misgiving about psychoanalysis as opposed to psychology, Mike and I are in very broad agreement: about understanding bowlers (p47) and the belief systems of batsmen (139); that thought is always helpful (p42); and that one cannot over communicate (p89). We similarly agree at the organisational level about the quality of Yorkshire's 1960s management that made Brian Close's captaincy's responsibilities "a mockery" (p53) and that manipulative management "the attempt to influence by subtle control in which the controller keeps the strings in his hands" is a poor technique (p171). I confess to a Brearley bias on cricket matters, that he prefers a third man (p183), abhors slow over rates (pp104-5), that weather forecasts should not be ignored (p111, pp145-6), and he even has far more positive things to say than nearly everyone else I've read about Geoffrey Boycott, including Geoffrey Boycott.

Assuming one is not a Test or County player, what still might be learned from 'The Art of Captaincy' is a start to a more rational approach to people as individuals operating in complex social and work environments which are both cooperative and competitive. Brearley's book is the best I've discovered on the psychology of cricket, but it stands out in a field of one, which is surprising when virtually every cricket commentary I hear frequently, if implicitly, discusses things of the mind. Psychology is often mentioned explicitly in commentaries as well, but with little or no understanding of the modern science of the mind that has been developed since the 1880s. There is a long educational road ahead when, returning to this chapter's opening paragraph, Geoffrey Boycott [6, p222] can proclaim, "I would not let a psychologist near my team.", before asking Simon Mann on Test Match Special, "Why do they need a psycho*analyst*?" (my emphasis).

[1] Festinger, L. (1957) *A Theory of Cognitive Dissonance.* Harper & Row.

[2] Brearly, M. (2001) *The Art of Captaincy.* Channel 4 Books: Macmillan.

[3] Hughes, S. (1997) *A Lot of Hard Yakka – Triumph and Torment: A County Cricketer's Life.* Headline.

[4] Simkins, M. (2007) *Fatty Batter: How Cricket Saved My Life (Then Ruined It).* Ebury Press.

[5] Morgan-Grenville, R. and Perkins, R. (2011) *Not Out First Ball: The Art of Being Beaten in Beautiful Places.* Bikeshed Books.

[6] Boycott, G. (2014) *Corridor of Certainty: My Life Beyond Cricket.* Simon & Schuster.

Chapter 22

The G.B. XI.

It wasn't until I'd started reading cricket books in earnest a couple of years before starting to draft this book that I discovered what fans who grew up with cricket do when there is no cricket. They'd construct fantasy teams that would satisfy some set of criteria, which might range from the reasonable to the eccentric: best ever Yorkshire XI; best post World War 2 left handed England Test XI; international XI of players who's first name starts with 'D', etc.

I tried it myself and can see the attraction, except there is no test of one's musings and I have no one to discuss such stuff with. I don't mind the latter. I quite liked the Richie Benaud [1] approach of choosing three teams, provided this is winnowed to a final eleven. Identifying 33 players, or 36 with a twelfth man, could itself be quite a challenge if one is too pernickety, or silly, about one's team selection criteria, e.g. a Sri Lankan international XI of players with five or fewer letter surnames?

Then one day in an idle lunch time I had the idea of a G.B. fantasy team, not Great Britain, but Geoff Boycott. At the time I was reading books by or about him. I greatly admire his complete dedication to cricket and see echoes of my own approach to my research career, I used to work more than eighty hours a week, fifty two weeks of the year, and my life was my work. Allowed to, Geoff and I would most happily talk about our work. So why not a team of twelve Geoffrey Boycotts? What a Good idea. Look at all the advantages of having a team of a dozen of the boogers.

So, off to Honest John's[40] to order the clones.

Being retired, I could only afford the clones in basic green. A team of green Geoff Boycotts I thought not inappropriate, provide it was the green of naivety, 'green' being short for 'greenhorn', and not the green of envy or environmentalism. As Leo McKinstry [3, p246] wrote of the original, pink Boycott, "In many ways, he was a curiously naïve figure … he had never managed to understand the easy compromises and deceptions that run through most human interactions." I'll hold my hand up to this; within my strictly applied ethical system I've an acquired allergy to liars.

The advantage of modern cloning technology, even of the budget variety, is that one doesn't have to wait twenty years for the things to grow up, and one can program in basic properties, knowledge and skills. So I ordered half the clones as left handers, not trusting to ambidexterity on my budget.

Geoffwun was to be closest to the pink'un and would open the batting with the left handed Geofftoo. After these platform building batsmen, Geofftrey would follow the loss of the first wicket, either following the opening style or, with a "sufficient" first partnership score, start to increase the run rate. Geoffaw, a left handed, elegant stroke maker would take the attack to the opposition with Geoffvee and the left handed Geoffmax, the two all rounders coming in before Geoffsven, the wicket keeper batsman. Of course the tail of the G.B. XI can bat, and the pace attack of Geoffate, Geoffnin (left arm seam) and Geoffecks is complimented by the medium fast Geoffmax. Similarly, the left arm leg spin of Geoffteem is supported by the right armed all rounder Geoffvee's finger spin. That was the plan for the perfect team, although I'm not sure about the spinners, is it better to have a right or left handed leg spinner, and *vice versa* for the finger merchant? Well, they'll just have to bowl around the

---

[40] For background details see [2].

wicket as needs requires.

One major advantage is that the G.B. XI are an economy team, as none of them drink, smoke and all go to bed early for their eight and a half hours uninterrupted slumber. Furthermore, these are players so are not spoiled by later media millions and, being fastidious eaters, even their food, being fresh and wholesome, is cheap. The clothes bill will come as a bit of a shock however, but the business acumen of Geoffdoz (twelfth man, all rounder, substitute wicket keeper and coach) should allow him to negotiate decent discounts when buying suits by the dozen.

Nets are interesting for the G.B. XI. Four wickets and the bowlers, two per wicket, take their full run up, as similar in every way to a match as possible, and they go on for hours, and hours, and hours.

It's not going to be all sweetness and light owning a dozen Geoff Boycotts, particularly green ones. It would probably be impossible to find a lower concentration of social skills in any dozen organisms on the other side of reality. On the other hand, they all start out with the same base level and are in complete agreement with themselves that what they are fanatically dedicated to is becoming better cricketers, no matter how good they are already. When one does get out in a match, at least he can go and sit in the dressing room with a towel over his head for a couple of hours as there are plenty more where he came from.

Bowling Boycotts are not implausible if the extreme dedication is programmed that way and, after all, the pink Boycott did bowl, taking 3 for 47 for England versus South Africa at Cape Town, 6th. January, 1965 [4]. With apologies for being personal, from photographs from his playing days I always though Geoff had a bit of a bowler's bum, or as P.G. Wodehouse might describe it, being somewhat callipygous [41]. Similarly, and as further

---

[41] "having well-shaped buttocks" – Concise Oxford English Dictionary, 7th. ed.

evidence of talent, the original Boycott did improve his fielding considerably once this was pointed out to him as a weakness when he was a young man [3]. As to who would captain my G.B. XI, I'm leaving considering that issue for some future rain interval.

I'd match my G.B. XI against any other fantasy team, on any wicket. We'll win because we are dedicated and won't be distracted. Except by the women, but, with the number required, green ones will just have to do.

[1] Benaud, R. (2005) *My Spin on Cricket.* Hodder & Stoughton.

[2] Holt, T. (2002) *Falling Sideways.* Orbit.

[3] McKinstry, L. (2005) *Geoff Boycott: A Cricketing Hero.* HarperSport: HarperCollins.

[4] Boycott, G. (1987) *Boycott: The Autobiography.* Macmillan.

Chapter 23

Meet Rab.

I'd like to introduce you to my mate rab – run-a-ball. Rab's a white ball cricket chap and a bit tardy, really only coming into play in the second innings.

I invented my rab method, which is not to claim that I was the first, but only that I sorted it out for myself. Indeed, it is common for live cricket commentators to say something like, "They now need a run a ball." What I have done is to work out how best to use rab, which I've never heard or read of.

In single innings cricket, Twenty20 or fifty overs as played internationally, and for the England and Wales Counties it became fifty overs in 2014, the challenge is to know how the team batting second is progressing relative to the first innings' total. On television during the second innings it is common for the score strap line at the bottom of the screen to regularly report the runs needed to win with so many overs or balls remaining.

To interpret the runs-in-balls-remaining metric during a match one needs a statistical model. It might surprise some that as a scientist I'd be seriously suspicious of a statistical model based on previous match data. I am so suspicious because I know how difficult and complicated analytical statistical testing can be, even when used to analyse carefully controlled laboratory experiments. Certainly over my decades of refereeing research papers, I've sent at least a couple of dozen back not recommending publication until the statistics were improved. What cricket commentators and numerate aficionados do is to use heuristic models (see Chapter 14) to interpret the state of a match from the numbers they have available to them.

A heuristic model is based on skill, knowledge, expertise, experience and, what is horribly called, "a gut feeling". In a fairly clear case, needing 48 runs to win in the last 3 overs, nearly everyone will back the defending team to win and the obvious, associated comment is that the team batting second needs 16 runs an over. Similarly, most of us would usually fancy the chances of the chasing team winning if they only need 18 runs in 3 overs. An exception to the latter example's expectation would be where the chasing team have lost all their main batsmen and the final tail are known rabbits with batting averages in single figures. Both these examples' interpretation use heuristic modelling, the expectations are hardly controversial, but, of course, they can occasionally turn out to be wrong.

Indeed, a few days before drafting this chapter I'd watched on the television a Champions League Twenty20 match where the chasing team won by making 45 runs in the last two overs! It ruined the match for me as it made the preceding three hours of play, which I had been analysing, as I always do in limited overs cricket, pretty much meaningless. I admit it was exciting cricket, but I'm less sure it was Good Cricket (Chapter 10).

Mentioned above is another measure of second innings progress, that of the required run rate. This is used often by radio commentators and is also usually provided with reasonable frequency within television's score strap line. It's major advantage is that it can be usefully used throughout a limited overs match's second innings. It is also useful in the first innings because the heuristic criteria are relatively simple, although they do differ for twenty20 and fifty overs cricket.

In current, fifty overs matches an overall run rate of 6 runs per over gives a final score of 300, which in top quality international matches would usually be reckoned a winning one, but one which still could be chased down. In contrast, in Twenty20 at the same level, the same run rate, leading to a total of only 120 runs, would hardly ever be defended successfully. A more realistic target to defend in Twenty20 would be a 180 score, i.e. a run rate of 9 runs per over. If I didn't do my own analyses, then required run rate is what I'd use.

A third measure of relative innings progress is the graphic "worm". This shows each team's cumulative score, plotting overs on the horizontal axis and runs scored so far on the vertical axis. Note, the alternative "skyscraper" graph, which shows runs scored in each over, is rarely used to compare the two teams, but usually is used to show one team's performance during their innings. For this reason this histogram is not discussed further here.

The problem with the worm graph is that to properly interpret it one needs to examine gradients. The graph is unnecessary just to report whether one team is ahead or behind the other team's run rate, which is why the graph's understanding requires inspecting gradients. To explain with a simple example, if in a Twenty20 match after ten overs the second team batting has the same run rate as the first team after ten overs[42], then how well the second team are doing will depend on the gradient of the first batting team's final ten overs. If the graph gets very much steeper, then the chasing team might be judge to be behind, but if it flattens out, then they would usually be judged to be ahead. Such judgements, as always, being modified by the number, and when, wickets are lost.

Unless one has had some appropriate training, then judging graphical gradients is not something people immediately do, if they do it at all. Furthermore, there are limits to graphics presented on television, not only of resolution (e.g. the size of characters and thickness of lines), but also the shape of the two dimensional space available limits the shape of the graph. To my expert eye the usual television worm graph needs to be taller to make

[42] i.e. both team's graphs share a single point, they cross or are coextensive, lying on top of each other.

relevant gradient changes better standout. Those using wide screen television formats are particularly disadvantaged; how the wealthy suffer!

Recently, I first came across it in 2013, there is the WASP (Winning And Score Predictor). This is just a single percentage figure that claims to predict which side will win. Details are readily available on the internet: the WASP was developed by Dr. Seamus Hogan and his graduate student Scott Brooker at the University of Canterbury and first used by Sky Sports (New Zealand) in 2012, and Wikipedia even provides the equation the WASP uses for its "dynamic programming". Designed as an alternative to the Duckworth-Lewis Method[43], it is no more comprehensible to cricket commentators and I was still hearing commentators on the radio late in the 2014 County season still asking what was the WASP.

I don't like it. I don't like the WASP because it discourages audience tactical and strategic thinking during a match, which is an activity which gives me considerable pleasure during all types of cricket. Basically, following just the single WASP figure discourages consideration of alternative possibilities for the rest of a match, whether a couple of quick wickets fall, or a decent batting partnership develops, or even that weather or bad light might intervene. I'd only be interested in the WASP if I had access to it interactively, in real-time, and could easily set up future scenarios such as a couple of quick wickets in the next five overs.

Howsoever complicated the WASP equation looks to those not of a mathematical bent, it's actually pretty simple and, therefore, no matter how computationally sophisticated, it provides only a simplified model of a particular match. If others find it useful, gives them a little pleasure, or whatever, then that is fine by me. For me, however, the WASP is misguided in that it addresses the

---

[43] DL does provide quite a good way of comparing each team's progress, but currently it is rarely provided during commentaries.

wrong question. I have doubts about predicting which side will win a match, as is often said, "It's a funny old game.", or as Durham's Captain, Paul Collingwood, oft remarked in interviews I heard in 2014, "That's just cricket." Instead of predicting which team will win, I want to know how the side batting second is doing so far in a limited overs match, which brings me on to rab.

The fundamental premise behind rab is that in white ball cricket the expectation is that there will on be six runs scored in every over[44]. In fifty overs cricket this would give a team 300 runs in their innings, which is a seriously good score. In Twenty20 it would give an innings total of 120, which is a poor score. This doesn't matter.

The way rab works is that at the end of the first innings a score is posted that is expressed as run-a-ball plus or minus so many runs. If the first inning score is 170, then in Twenty20 this would be rab+50 [45] and in 50 overs cricket it would be rab–130. During a second innings rab is just the number of runs still needed minus the current number of second innings balls remaining. As mentioned above, this information is frequently available in the television strap line so all that is required is a simple subtraction, e.g. 57 runs needed with 32 balls remaining is rab+25 (57 – 32 = 25); if this tasks you abilities at mental arithmetic then the WASP is probably your best bet. It's hardly more difficult with just the radio provided one can remember the first innings total; write it down if your memory is frail, I do. What I actually do is to keep a mental running count of the rab score, updating it at the end of each over, if not more frequently within an over; it depends on the match situation.

As an example, if in a Twenty20 match the team

---

[44] The reason for using one run a ball as the base measure is that it makes computation particularly easy as six balls in the over is equivalent to six runs and the two are thus interchangeable.

[45] 170 inninings_score – (6 runs_per_over x 20 overs) = 170 – 120 = 50.

batting first score 165 runs, then how are the team batting second doing if the have a score at the end of the power play overs (six overs bowled) of 40 runs?

Well? 40 runs in 6 overs chasing 165. Is this: bad, poor, O.K., satisfactory, or good? Is the answer obvious? It is if you use my rab method.

The chasing team start their innings with a score of rab+45 (165 – 120 = 45)[46]. After six overs they have achieved rab+41. This is not a big difference to where they started. Therefore, the team batting second are doing poorly.

It is possible to make calculating the rab score after six overs look complicated:

$$45 - (40 - (6 \times 6)) = 45 - (40 - 36) = 45 - 4 = 41$$

In fact it is incredibly easy to calculate in several ways. Above, it's just the current score (40) minus the balls bowled (6 x 6 = 36) and then the result (4) is subtracted from the original rab score (45) to give rab+41. The simpler way is to subtract balls remaining from the runs still required.

In fact, even easier still, during a match I just remember the last rab score at the end of an over and just deduct or add the number of runs scored in the next over minus six. So, for the team chasing 165, if they had 30 runs after 5 overs (still rab+45) and score 10 runs in the sixth over, then in that over the have reduced their rab from rab+45 to rab+41.

When I'm really interested, then I just keep mentally updating the rab score after each ball bowled. This is very straightforward as a dot ball increases rab by one, a single doesn't change rab, two runs decreases rab by one, … and a four reduces rab by three. Once you get used to it, it really is very easy and it is much harder to describe than to

---

[46] In Twenty20 cricket the run-a-ball score is always 120 (6 runs an over times 20 overs.)

do.

To clinch the argument for using rab, consider the alternative, the run rate required, for the same example. After five overs the chasing team have a required run rate of 9:

$$\frac{\text{165 target} - \text{30 scored}}{\text{20 overs} - \text{5 bowled}} = 135/15 = 9$$

After the sixth over the required run rate has hardly changed at 8.9:

$$\frac{\text{165 target} - \text{40 scored}}{\text{20 overs} - \text{6 bowled}} = 125/14 = 8.928$$

While I can divide 135 by 15 in my head, 135 being a fortuitous number, I don't know my 14 times table, so it is out with the calculator. The problem is simply that long division is very difficult to do mentally. In contrast, calculating rab requires just simple addition and subtraction, and perhaps knowing one's six times table (to calculate the number of balls remaining).

In addition, rab is actually the more sensitive measure, as is illustrated in the example above. Practically, there is no difference between 9 and 8.9, but, with the good sixth over for the batsmen, rab reflects this by dropping from 45 to 41, which, I can see at a glance, is a drop of just under 10% (9.11% by calculator).

While talking of a typical Twenty20 match is probably statistical nonsense, rab does help identify typical passages of play. As illustrated above, in the first six overs when fielding restrictions are fiercest, then a team doing well should expect rab to reduce by a dozen or so[47]. Rab is particularly good at identifying quiet passages of play, and these do occur in Twenty20 cricket, often in the middle overs: spin and change bowlers come into play, the ball

---

[47] 8 runs per over will reduce rab by 12 in six overs: (8rpo – 6@rab) x 6overs = rab–12.

does change a little, batsmen have just come to the crease, and so forth.

There are times when live commentators, who don't use rab, and I disagree. They may suggest that a team is batting satisfactorily, say getting seven runs and over, but five overs of this will reduce rab by only five, which is not much if the current rab is in the thirties or forties. When rab seesaws it can be particularly informative and I often have thoughts such as, "Now they are back to a rab they had three overs ago!" It's much harder to see this with the smaller changes in the required run rate and the runs-in-so-many-balls metric doesn't immediately convey the rab sort of information at all.

Rab works equally well with fifty over cricket, although I tend to calculate it less frequently since scoring is slower than in Twenty20. The range of rab numbers is different since in fifty overs a good score at a run a ball is 300. Quite often the starting rab is negative, e.g. a first innings score of a defendable 280 is rab–20. How one interprets rab is the same as in Twenty20, however, because one focuses on changes to rab rather than on its absolute value. As such, it provides a simple way to in effect examine the gradient changes on the worm graph described earlier in this chapter.

I recommend rab to you. How more convincing can I be? If I have nearly convinced you, then try using rab for several matches. It'll take a couple for you to get used to using rab, and is easiest to start with television and the information in the score strap line. Remember, rab's just runs needed minus balls left in the innings. Go on, try it.

Chapter 24

Mad Advertising.

When I have only a live internet video stream on my television to watch a cricket match, I am happy to accept the adverts as the price I pay for my free access.

Starting with the bizarre, when I log in to every live stream I have to fight up to half a dozen pop-up adverts, which one has to close one way or another. Nearly all have false close icons [X], but the best of these liars fire their advertising window, I close them down on a real window's [X], and they disappear. Also, I've learned to recognise on many servers where the hidden, real close window [X]'s are on the adverts.

On a technical observation, each of my three main computers handles the adverts from the same website differently. The importance of this observation is that there are quite a lot of websites which do not allow you to watch the live cricket stream because, a couple of tens of seconds after access, the web window will switch to an advert which cannot be closed or recovered from. This is insane! The adverts pay for the cricket, but if I can't see the cricket, then I won't see the adverts. I cry pestilence, "You brass studs!", on the advertisers that cut to their website and completely prevent me watching the cricket on that particular server.

For years I could not understand how those in charge of these servers, businessmen, who want, neigh need, for people to see their clients' adverts, could allow their advertisers to subvert their website so that watching cricket on it is impossible. I am slightly more reasonable in my criticism having seen how differently the adverts are handled by my three main computers, each with different

Microsoft operating systems (from XP to 8.01). However, my "slightly more reasonable" doesn't prevent me from thinking that technologically it sucks, and I'm pretty disgusted at the lack of the most basic software engineering testing; it's only a website so hardly difficult stuff for even a third rate usability expert to sort out.

Once I've caught a live, reliable, video cricket stream, then there are the adverts as one gets on all commercial television. I never, ever listen to adverts on television. By mouse or TV remote I immediately mute them, always. I do see television adverts, and I've been interested in them, from about their video technology to their cross cultural differences, for decades.

Three decades ago we, the beautiful Japanese wife and I, had a ridiculously expensive Panasonic VCR (Video Cassette Recorder) which could play both European and Japanese format video tapes. Our regular Red Cross parcels from Japan, sometimes opened by Her Majesty's Customs Officers because their dogs probably weren't keen on the dried seaweed, fish, mushrooms, crackers and similar edible exotica, now would also contain video tapes of hours, and hours, of Japanese (junk?) television. It was great after the daughter was born because, trying to give her the bilinguility gift, from the videos she had a lot of passive second language exposure, some adult stuff (not in the sexual sense) and hours of children's cartoons in Japanese, often the same programmes that were dubbed into English on the BBC and ITV[48].

Thirty years ago, I thought the Japanese adverts were terrible. I thought they were crude, resembling the British advertising of the 1960s, at best, which is a pretty bad, even at best. It's not a very sophisticated sociological idea to suggest that interesting and informative metrics of a culture might come from assessing its commercial television advertising. I can think of much to commend the idea, for example, that a country's domestic

---

[48] This is long before Freeview, satellite, cable, etc.

commercial advertising is written for their home audience, to influence and sell them things, and are not really for an international audience. Which would you trust more, an analysis of such adverts or what the politicians, diplomats and their spin doctors tell us about their country and its international relationships?

I'd noticed Pakistan Television's development of advertising in recent years, but for a decade I've been impressed with much of the Indian television advertising, a bit different but certainly on a par with the British advertising I'm too familiar with. I think the test is humour, and I've seen excellent jokes on Indian TV, which don't need language, which is clever in a "linguistically diverse" country (about 800 languages?), and I've the mute on anyway.

An example that sticks in my mind, for 'Mentos' or something sweets, is of a teenage lad on a scooter who sees the police stopping riders for not wearing a motorcycle helmet. He gets a watermelon from a stall and cuts it out to make a helmet and so rides, smug faced, past the bemused, stumblebum policemen. Jolly funny, for an advert. On the other hand, I'm not sure this advert would be generally approved of in the oh so free U.K. What does it tell us about the relationship between jolly, successful young society and society's official guardians, the perhaps not so jolly police? India and England are grossly different societies, whatsoever our brief Imperial entwinement. Great big, gross cultural differences are hard to fathom, or climb beyond, because the gap is just so big. Perhaps, I think, one can judge better, get a better handle on cultural differences, by looking at some of their similar minutiae, for example, their commercial television advertising.

Mad advertising? Poor 'Claim Time Solicitors' who paid to advertise during the Pakistan versus New Zealand ODI in Sharjar, Friday 12th. December, 2014. From my start time, 11am GMT, their single, brief, twenty second slot advert was repeated at the end of every over. Every over!

It wasn't even a mildly exciting advert, just being a modestly attractive young lass, no doubt supposedly looking intelligent and trustworthy, giving a brief punt for her solicitor's products.

In my youth of anger, actually most of my life, I would have cursed at the ridiculous, lousy repetition of the same rotten advert. In my grumpy dotage, I was never middle-aged, I feel sorry for Claim Time Solicitors who I think were ripped off. How much did they pay? With wickets falling, drinks and other intervals, their advert must have been shown, alone and without any competition, about hundred times during the day. It made them look like complete idiots, and idiots who don't care about cricket, which they interrupt without sympathy or consideration at every over's end. I'm sure no one would mind their advert, rotten or not, after every three or four overs, as I said at the beginning, it's advertising that gives us all television cricket, but they were poorly advised. As Gideon Haigh [1, p143] describes the downside of brand recognition over exposure in televised cricket, "it stirs irritation and objection, as a result, perhaps, of incessant, cloying, annoying repetition."

To combat the advert-every-over approach of PTV, I often try to use an alternative stream. The cricket is identical, but other providers will show the score card or other useful data between overs, without any commentary. There are times, however, when the alternative stream will cut out too frequently whereas, at least when Pakistan are playing, PTV is very reliable. Image quality isn't very good on PTV compared to many other servers, but this is a minor concern to me. My point is that PTV is often my last resort because of their advertising policy.

Advertising, particularly on television, is what fuels the vast wealth that has been created in cricket, led by India, in recent years. For international matches, anyone with an internet connection can usually access at least a dozen competing servers that provide exactly the same video and commentary feed of the cricket, but vary in their advertising, between and, even, during overs. Not being a businessman, I am perplexed that more care has not yet been taken with advertising policy if, as with me, viewers will choose which server, and hence which adverts they see, depending principally on how intrusive the adverts are to watching the cricket.

Admittedly, most of the advertising is for local consumption. On the other hand, many products, from mobile phones to paint, chocolate and some movies, to give just a few examples, are available in many countries, including the U.K. I wonder if the internet based, global advertising market has been fully considered and, at present, whether it is under exploited. A case in point where it does work currently is in financial services, particularly money transfer to the subcontinent. It isn't implausible to suggest that the direct advertising market is not those in Asia, but those working abroad who wish to send money home.

Advertising to the at-home Asians requires an additional step between advertiser and market, either influencing someone who then goes abroad, or requiring an advert's message to be passed on to those already abroad. From an advertising point of view, this sort of delay or secondary linkage is not desirable.

While it was PTV that stimulated me to think about television advertising and cricket, my comments are intended generally and I've a vested interest in that better thought out advertising policies should lead to less interrupted cricket watching.

Chasing over 250, New Zealand won easily with four overs to spare.

[1] Haigh, G. (2010) *Sphere of Influence: Writings on Cricket and its Discontents*. Simon & Schuster.

Chapter 25

The Emancipation of our Cousins.

Obviously our species, *Homo Sapiens*, have found many disgusting, immoral ways to discriminate against our fellows. Goodness, and very depressingly, there are millions of people who are simply slaves, even today! Our own discriminated against include women, children, the disabled, aged, people who don't have unattractive splodgy pink skin, the differently gendered, belonging to a different wrong religion, those who live outside of Greater London, Yorkshire or, in the Neolithic, on the hill next door. We have more poor and dispossessed, I think, than any civilisation should possess. In the deepest depths of my despair, I do doubt my willingness to confess my species.

A positive thing, apparently undisputed, is that Geoffrey Boycott is "colour blind" (e.g. [1]), which is not about ignoring skin colour but about accepting cultural differences. I too am without prejudice.

I am without prejudice. A voracious reader even as a young child, around ten years old I discovered Science Fiction (SF). I'd emptied the local library of such before my dozenth birthday. My current SF library, my third, is about 3,000 books; I've not bought many recently. The idea of non-human intelligence is thus one I've been familiar with for all of my teenage and adult (qualifying on years, anyway) life. Happy with enjoying the concepts of extraterrestrial intelligence, I suspect I do a better speculative job than SF writers, my own science and engineer research and teaching has involved considerations of human, animal and machine intelligences. Thus, on Sunday, 14th. December, 2014, as Pakistan in their third ODI against New Zealand, batting first, demolished, destroyed, and decimated the bowling, my idle mind was crossed by an idea of delight.

"A monkey would have caught that!", not that Pakistan gave New Zealand many chances. What sort of sociological engineering techniques could have the potential to integrate the 'lower orders' into an equitable, safe society? Never mind all the horrible inter-human nastiness, how could one make our close cousins[49], say chimpanzees, members of our mixed culture?

The Roman Empire had a good idea. A quarter of a century or so as a lowly legionnaire and you got to be a Citizen of Rome, with massive subsequent advantages for your family. A thousand years or so of recent European history, however, doesn't support the notion that those of the lowest military ranks, who survive, are subsequently well treated. Nor have things much improved in our modern world, as exemplified in the U.K. by the need for an ex-services' charity like 'Help for Heroes' or the campaign, fronted by the gorgeous actress Joanna Lumley, to improve the lot of Britain's retired Ghurkha troops. As Kipling put it in his poem 'Tommy':

> *For it's Tommy this, an' Tommy that, an*
> *"Chuck him out, the brute!"*
> *But it's "Saviour of 'is country" when the guns*
> *begin to shoot;*

So if a lowly military route to cultural integration isn't an option, what of that other arm of Victorian Imperialism, cricket? Why not cricketing chimpanzees? And, why not, playing along side those under muscled bean poles with short arms?

One's on an intellectual sticky wicket to say that chimpanzees are quite intelligent. Even with humans the

---

[49] The 'Great Apes', family *Hominidae*, consists of us humans, plus chimpanzees, bonobos, gorillas and orangutans.

concept eludes us and psychometrics, the measurement of minds, uses an operational definition (see Chapter 8): intelligence tests measure what intelligence tests measure. Even so, I recall a seminar from my Cambridge University days (1977-82) where the proposal was that relative inter-species intelligence could be estimated by deviations from the brain size to body mass ratio. Basically, an organism with a big body needs a big brain to control it, so, that elephants have bigger brains that humans, doesn't make them more intelligent. The telling data instead involves dividing brain size by body size, where humans, and their great ape cousins, win out over the large bodied elephants and most other creatures. I don't think it is just a case of, "Well, the humans would say that."

Chimpanzees are certainly capable of learning language. They don't have the throat for speech, but they can be taught Amerslang, the American sign language used by deaf humans. Many animals have quite sophisticated means of communication, but what distinguishes language from mere communication is syntax (a.k.a. grammar). In a language the order of the symbols determines meaning, so the sentences, 'The batsman hit the ball.' and 'The ball hit the batsman.' have radically different meanings although using the same symbols (words). There is a vast amount of research on primate psychology and their language capabilities, but the bottom line is that if you let them speak with their hands, then you can chat to a chimpanzee, at least in a similar way as you can chat to a child.

Chimpanzees are social animals, it has been suggested that this is why they need over sized brains relative to the size of their bodies. They also indulge in play and games, so if children can play cricket, why not chimpanzees?

A gentleman shouldn't mention the New Zealand score (22 for 2 after 5 overs chasing Pakistan's 364 for 7 in their 50 overs), but as the match went on with its one sided, dreary destruction (it wasn't 'Good Cricket – Chapter 10), I started to list the strengths, and weaknesses, of top class chimpanzee cricketers.

Bowling! Chimpanzees aren't as tall as many humans, not forgetting that Pakistan's Mohammad Irfan, who was playing while I was making my notes, is seven foot one (or two), but what long arms they've got. Imagine, a seriously fast chimpanzee knuckle running to the crease and whipping a jaffa from the top of that long straight arm. It would be like using one of those devices people use to throw balls to dogs (and sometimes to cricketers in training). If a chimpanzee could do it at all, then 100mph+ balls could be a regular thing.

I'm not sure whether chimpanzees could learn to become extreme fast bowlers, but what spin bowlers they'd be. Never mind their gait, they wouldn't need any run up. Their fingers are perfect for spin bowling with long and very strong fingers covered in a skin, superior to the human, for spin bowling purposes. I reckon they'd get more revolutions on the ball than any human, perhaps twice that of all but the best of the human lot.

Many human spin bowlers have been number eleven batsmen, so a chimpanzee spinner would be in good historical company even if weak with the bat. Could chimpanzees bat? They've got excellent hand-eye coordination and certainly the arm leverage to hit massive sixes. They aren't very tall, so wouldn't be bothered by short pitched bowling. I'm not so sure they'd be that good running between the wickets for quick runs.

As fielders, I'd put any chimpanzees in a team near to the bat and leave fielding in the deep to the truly bipedal people. Perhaps three human slip catchers could be covered by two chimpanzee slips because, with their arms, they wouldn't have to stand so close together. As a wicket keeper, a chimpanzee might be pretty good up to the stumps, but I'm not so sure about when standing back; could they make their equivalent of the tall human's outstretched dive?

I can genuinely cheer myself up by imaging the antics of triumph when a cricketing chimpanzee took a wicket, a catch, or hit a six. The waving, clapping and high fives would be extraordinary, on-field and in the crowd, but both chimpanzees and humans would have to learn the meaning of their different facial expressions. It's pretty odd that humans show their teeth when very happy, for most others it's meaning is aggressive, no laughing matter.

On the downside, what about the smell? I make the usual response to this, the chimpanzees will just have to learn to put up with it. The chimpanzees will probably want to help their human team mates with their grooming, they are fastidious. In the longer term, I look forward to the battles with MCC to allow all *hominidea* membership. Will it be harder than allowing women in? What would it do to the MCC dress code?

One has just got to accept the human hypocrisy, another black mark for homo sapiens, of Pelham Warner's words compared to the on-field bodyline deeds of 1932 (e.g. [2]). The West Indies provide a better example of how cricket can support, if not lead, cultural change, as expounded, for example, by C.L.R. James [3]. Learie Constantine, one of the great West Indian cricketers, became a member of the House of Lords, which was good progress given the racism in Britain against those with more attractive skin colours than its Anglo-Saxon and Norman descendents. Could one of our cousins, once their cricket playing days are done, be similarly elevated?

I'm not naïve enough to suppose that if we could expand the people franchise to include all the great apes, that this wouldn't just give the current humans more people to be horrible to. I'll be sorry when, inevitably, chimpanzees learn of warfare. I'd admire them if they told the lanky streaks to shove it. Indeed, let those idiots learn from chimpanzee culture.

I've got no problems with having a couple of pints in the pub with a chimpanzee. Fortunately, I've no pretence at any arm wrestling capability. Let's see how good the bugger is at darts after a quart of strong real English ale.

[1] McKinstry, L. (2005) *Geoff Boycott: A Cricketing Hero*. HarperSport – HarperCollins.

[2] Frith, D. (2003) *Bodyline Autopsy*. ABC Press.

[3] James, C.L.R. (1963) *Beyond a Boundary*. Yellow Jersey Press (2005).

Chapter 26

The St. Benaud Heresy.

"Don't speak unless you can add to the picture."

The BBC started television cricket coverage in 1938 and the above quote is attributed to Seymour de Lotbiniere (circa 1946) as the "the most important part" of his "Pyramid method" according to Richie Benaud [1, p16]. Others agree that historically the BBC is to blame, but I blame St. Benaud.

Most revered of cricket commentators, sainthood becomes him and, with millions of followers over the years, mere miracles must be easy to come by for Richie Benaud's fans. Miracles here don't include England winning The Ashes, but fortuitous events must have occurred to some of St. Benaud's devotees while listening to him; the miraculous to others being their misperception of probability to me.

I blame St. Benaud for his widespread promulgation of the BBC creed that cricket commentary should not describe what can been seen on television, but should only add what viewers can't see. Unchanged, the St. Benaud legacy remains a global phenomenon to this day. I don't like it, I disagree with him, and I'm prepared to risk the hate mail, trolls and assorted beastliness that his misguided disciples may direct at me. I'm sure Richie wouldn't approve of such behaviour, what might be done in His name, but, " Jesus!", wasn't it ever thus?

Seventy years ago domestic television was seen as a wondrous thing, but what was seen was not much in the tiny, low quality black-and-white screens of the day. Valves and cathode ray guns, forsooth! Seen as wondrous, however, I imagine that back then people really did watch television, they looked at the images intensely, which they probably needed to do given the quality, or lack of it, that was offered. Radio was already a familiar domestic technology so it was the addition of moving images that was at the core of the TV revolution in home entertainment. That was then, but my thesis is that: (a) the world has moved on; and (b) the BBC, and hence St. Benaud, were in any case wrong.

What about blind people? Television cricket commentary is absolute rubbish if you can't see the screen. That this is deliberately so, once as a matter of BBC policy and now, apparently, as an unquestioned universal belief amongst cricket commentators, must be against all recent anti-discrimination legislation. I have no idea who the visually handicapped should sue, but I wish them well in any class action they might attempt in the courts.

Originally, cricket on television was a single camera affair. I don't know about other televised sports during television's early era, but the size of a cricket field is such that much of relevance to the cricket viewer will be off-camera. It might be argued that using a camera in a single location is just the same as someone who was watching at the ground. Not so!

What we see, a percept, is entirely a construction of our mind's mental processes based on extremely limited and poor quality information provided by our eyes. Camera optics are enormously superior to those of our eyes, but cameras have a very narrow field of view and must obey optical laws, a geometry of the straight lines that light travels, which means that distant objects are very small and near ones very large.

It is easy to demonstrate to oneself the difference between normal human visual perception and what is offered by a camera: hold a toilet roll tube up to one eye, cover the other, and look at some distant scene. You'll find that you'll have to move your head around a lot. In contrast, what we normally see is a stable world, out there, which subtends around 120 degrees of visual angle, one third of a circle centred on your head.

The percept is a remarkable thing and for most of human history it has been wrongly confused with reality, whereas we now understand that it is the result of some very sophisticated mental information processing. The eyes are always moving and the percept is constructed, and then, importantly, maintained, based on a tiny part of the scene that is roughly in focus in the eyes[50], and a massive, greatly blurred surround.

Attention, the allocation of mental processing resources (see Chapter 8), allows us to look at something, say the batsman at the crease, and he will look larger than predicted by optical laws and we will add detail, not from our eyes, but from what we know based on previous visual experience, mostly unconscious beliefs, and so forth.

Looking at the batsman, we still, in some sense, see the deep fielders far from the batsman, although our mind has scant evidence from the eyes. The visual perception system compensates for this state of affairs in several ways, for example, by cleverly being sensitive to motion, particularly unexpected motion, so if a deep fielder moves, then the eyes will move to provide better visual evidence of the changed state and cause that part of the percept to be updated.

Television can't do any of the many tricky things that our minds do, so watching at a cricket ground, even though only from one location, is very different from what can be seen from a single television camera. Watching inter-War film footage, admittedly a lot can be done with one camera by using pan and zoom, but it isn't like

---

[50] The fovea, where the image is best, albeit poorly, in focus, subtends about 4 degrees of visual angle. If you fully extend your arm and hold up you thumb, the width of your thumb nail is about two degrees of visual angle. You'd need something of much smaller diameter than a toilet roll tube to simulate just how narrow is our eye's view of the world, even though our mind's view is 120 degrees.

watching with the mind's eye at the ground.

Today television uses many cameras and levels of zoom undreamed of in the 1930s. Even so, it still failed my test. What I tried to do was to establish all the fielding locations as I do when watching cricket on the radio. I found it hard to do with television for fielders in the deep, until the ball approaches them. I realised that usually I don't even bother to try to locate the deep fielders when I'm watching cricket on television, and I assume that's the case for most people. Trying to locate them, I found myself concentrating on the few seconds of wider angled shots that one gets relatively infrequently on modern televised cricket. It was a lot of effort, it made watching the rest of the televised match difficult, but it does illustrate a profound difference in content between radio commentary and what can be seen on television, even today.

In my experience, every radio cricket commentator always and regularly informs listeners of the fielding positions. In my experience, television cricket commentators rarely report the whole field, but will comment on individual fielding positions, particularly if they are unusual (e.g. fly slip) or controversial (e.g. no third man). Watch televised cricket with the sound off. Obviously, the commentators on the television's audio channel do provide a great deal of information. Of necessity, radio cricket commentators must provide much more.

I think a mistake has been made, an old BBC boo-boo promoted by St. Benaud. People can see less on television than its commentators believe. The commentators have a fine view of the ground and one or more live video feeds. The television viewer usually has but one video feed which chops between different cameras every few seconds. My feeling is that the television viewer is passive, being dragged around by only what is presented to see and what additional information the commentators provide. They, the producers and directors, a telling title, and commentators, not the viewers, are in control!

I'll happily admit that I don't like television. My objection is that it is cognitive resource greedy. While the human mind is a fantastically powerful information processing device, it is not unlimited. The task of watching television involves so much visual and language processing that there is no mental capacity left to do anything else. I believe this is why television watching is a passive activity, it requires so much mental activity that there's no scope for doing another parallel activity. Mentally, I'm a dynamic sort of chap and so don't like being led around like a pig with a ring through its nose.

What really annoys me about television, however, is that it is mentally undemanding. Many people think this about television's typical content, that it's dumbing down for the masses, etc., even with "serious" television. My objection is different: television is just so very slow.

Decades ago when Freeview was new and, suddenly, I had access to more than four channels, I spent some months watching several TV programmes in parallel. What I did was to programme a number of 'favourites' into my remote control and then keep pushing the cycle button. I found that I could watch up to four programmes at once when I cycled through programmes sufficiently quickly that an actor starting a sentence would be completing it after cycling through the three other channels. This is mentally exhausting, but it demonstrates that one does have spare mental capacity when television watching, even though it is hard to utilise. I can choose my reading speed, a junk Science Fiction paperback is but about three hours of entertainment, and I can stop and contemplate before returning to printed text. I really would rather read than watch television.

Back to cricket, for once I am in the majority camp. Against us all I found the following from Marcus Berkmann [1, p122] who suggests that those who prefer a radio commentary with the sound off on the television are "blind or a bit dim, but it would be hard to justify by any other criterion." He continues:

> *Let's grasp the full stupidity of the single, bloodcurdingly inane sentence. 'I always turn down the sound and listen to the radio instead.'*

Thank you for the humorous hyperbole, Marcus, but there are sound reasons why you are wrong and that you wrong us.

First, as argued above, the information content is greater in radio commentary than in a television one. Second, provided listening to the radio is the primary task and the television isn't watched continuously in parallel, then one has spare mental capacity for other tasks. Typically I'll use this spare capacity for mental arithmetic and similar activities that let me judge a cricket match's progress (Chapters 14 and 23). In 2014 I also spent much time making notes for this book while watching cricket on the radio. If I've only a televised match with its commentary, then, when I'm making notes, I simply miss the cricket, unless a major event like a wicket falling occurs, because there just isn't enough information content in the television's audio commentary when I am not looking at the screen.

That "I am not looking at the screen" encapsulates the Benaudian error. The BBC may have been right in the early days of domestic television, that people were prepared, even avid, to watch the television screen intensely. In our multimedia age I think the novelty has well worn off and television is now treated much more casually. If there is a video stream available, then it makes sense to have it on while still primarily following the cricket via the radio commentary because there is information on the video stream which even the radio commentators can't include.

I even quite like seeing a cricket ground, where the wicket is located on the square, how the outfield has been mown, the architecture, the surrounding countryside and the crowd, or lack of it in many places in the world. Mostly, though, all I want to do is to glance at the television occasionally, to check a particular shot against the radio commentary, to get data such as the score, overs bowled or left, and, to be boorishly repetitive, whether the facing batsman is right or left handed (Chapter 6 and *ibid.*).

Cross checking radio commentary against what the television shows raises the issue of the synchronisation between audio and video streams. Fortunately, the television always follows the radio, I can't remember a case of the reverse. The lag between the two can range from 2-3 seconds to 2-3 minutes. Anything over a couple of minutes, half an over, is pretty hopeless unless a major event, for example, a wicket falling or a third umpires review occurs, and one is prepared to wait for the television stream to catch up. My ideal is a lag of about three seconds. This lets me watch a ball bowled on the radio and, if sufficiently interesting, then I can glance at the television for, what is in effect, a replay of it. If it just passes through to the wicket keeper, then I don't bother with the delayed televised version of that ball. Even for spin bowlers, a lag of 20-30 seconds is O.K. as a four minute over rate means that a ball is bowled on average every half minute (allowing for a minute between overs).

A further advantage, to me at least, to having both radio commentary and a muted televised stream is that I don't have to keep muting the between overs television adverts. I don't care if the adverts are in English, Hindu, Urdu or whatever, I don't want to hear their inane jabbering, I can't stand it to be frank. Admittedly I've a highly practiced skill with carefully positioned TV remote or mouse so that muting the adverts hardly interrupts my thoughts, but it is better not to have to, often, keep on pushing a button.

I think that the BBC, St. Benaud, and all television's cricket commentators, are now wrong. Many people don't want to be locked into having to watch the television continuously. They, the providers, need a different model which is not dominated by the visual in television; a multimedia model where a highly descriptive audio stream is provided as the primary information source and the assumption is that people will often only glance at the screen. Television is no longer novel and what I am arguing for is a reconsideration, for cricket, of the prioritisation of the multimedia channels: I suggest giving the audio primacy over the pictures. While quoted as humorous [3, p133], Max Walker might be right and that, "One day there will be radio with pictures."

The lack of synchronisation between radio and television streams means that I've never experienced what I've suggested. As a final muse, since it takes some small time for a commentator to observe a ball bowled and then describe it, I wonder that with a more highly descriptive television commentary, whether it would be desirable to artificially add a lag to the television pictures, say of my "ideal" two or three seconds. A technical step too far, perhaps?

[1] Benaud, R. (2005) *My Spin on Cricket.* Hodder & Stoughton.

[2] Berkmann, M. (1995) *Rain Men.* Abacus.

[3] Croker, C. (2008) *Stumped! The World's Funniest Cricket Quotes.* Crombie Jardine.

Chapter 27

Ambitions Remaining.

Ambitions? Do I have any? Would I want some? For myself, probably not, but perhaps a few remain concerning this book. I've already had a successful international scientific career and I'm not the slightest bit interested in fame, and never have been. Standing up in front of hundreds of people at conferences was part of my job, but I travelled far less than other professors, I travelled reluctantly, and in retirement my personal preference would be to never travel more than a mile or so, on foot, from our family home in Bournemouth. No matter how many stars it might have, there is no hotel in the world that is more comfortable, for me, than my own home, which I see as a machine that has evolved, by design, for my own comfort; I've everything I want, in its proper, findable place. Really, I'm a marketing nightmare, I really don't want anything[51].

I never take holidays, I don't like them, and I almost feel sorry for people who want or need them: is their home, life and work so bad that they are desperate to escape, even for a fortnight or so? I don't want to see the world. Show me a supposedly pretty landscape and I'll speculate about the underlying geology, or the ecology, the prevailing meteorology, what are its systems, or some combination of such analyses. Mostly I'll be wondering when we can leave. My gravest concern about publishing 'Watching Cricket on the Radio' is that it will force me to

---

[51] I am reminded by the beautiful Japanese wife that we need to replace our 1960s kitchen, that the garden gates are completely rotten, etc., but I don't really want these, howsoever necessary.

travel, either to promote it or as a consequence of it. If you've read this and we subsequently meet, then I ask of a little sympathy as I am not going to like being away from home.

Economics provides an interesting view of the world, but I've no interest in money at the personal level. The beautiful Japanese wife looks after all money matters in our household, I just take out beer funds occasionally. As I understand it, we are pretty poor and we do need to have a lodger to make ends meet. So, yes, I do want this book to be successful and to make a modest profit. Even a handful of pounds would be welcome, particularly by the bJw. More importantly, any such profit means that people will have bought this book and, having paid, they may read it, and if they've read it, then, a smidgeon, they may have been entertained, educated and, although I think it unlikely, elevated by reading it.

The preface warns readers of my Reithian objectives, to entertain, educate and elevate. I suspect that mental and moral elevation is a long term thing for people and one little book can be no more than a small stimulus in much bigger systems.

Presumably every author of books for popular markets thinks that their book will be entertaining. Parent to their published prose, they are not to be trusted with evaluation of their progeny. As this book's author, at least I have explicitly considered whether my readership will be entertained by my efforts. I can only leave judgement to others of my success, but I'd settle for a tick in the 'satisfactory' box on entertainment value, although, naturally, wishing to do better for my baby.

Education! This would seem more my business. As a scientist and research engineer my job was to discover stuff and then to tell people about it. It was always about ethics, I wanted to develop and use my abilities to make the world a better place for people. I chose to do what I call "research engineering" because it would multiply my influence, hopefully for Good, so I built theories and methods that real engineers could then use to build things, mostly computers, based on my work. Quite deliberately I was a tool maker rather than tool user.

Goodness, why change a good thing, and a thing for Good, at my age? To be brutal, education is about deliberately changing people, how they think and what they do. Properly done, it involves an enormous moral responsibility. By design, 'Watching Cricket on the Radio' is an educational device. It is intended to improve the worlds of cricket. It is no typographic error, "worlds" is plural because my educational targets are multiple: cricket lovers, players, support staff, commentators, and a host of managers and administrators, of the game and its media presentation.

I have hopes. Finishing off this book I was encouraged by the following about good batsmen: "Their brain is like a machine calculating …"; "The computer inside the batsman's mind …"; and "All this computing going on in their mind …". The first two are from Angus (Gus) Fraser and the third was a reply from his co-commentator, Bob Willis, during the rain affected second day of the South Africa versus West Indies Test at St. George's Park, Port Elizabeth, December 27th., 2014. The match was finally abandoned due to a "wet outfield" on the final day.

I am encouraged because they have got the idea that the mind is an information processing device, as are computers. So over this first hurdle, the next is to clarify that they are using a metaphor. The third hurdle, a water jump, is that such metaphorical mental calculations are a functional specification, that the mind, somehow, must perform the equivalent to how things can be calculated using mathematics, and usually using computers to do the sums. The critical point is that biological computation uses different methods to achieve similar results to those of our computer assisted mathematics.

My standard example here involves hearing. I assume that most people are aware that complex sounds, such as speech and music, are made up of a mixture of fundamental frequencies and their harmonics. Such sounds can be analysed and their component frequencies unpacked using what is called a Fourier Transform and a decent computer, but this is in the domain of professional, expert mathematicians. The human system achieves a similar analysis by using an array of band pass filters and some specialised neural wiring. Basically, imagine a set of microphones that each respond to only a very narrow band of frequencies. Sound frequencies present will then be signalled by their corresponding microphone's output[52]. Admittedly the biological system is a lot more complicated than this, but the point is that it achieves a similar result as applying the Fourier Transform equations to the same sound.

We are a long way from understanding the phenomenally complicated biological calculations involved in the visual processing of fast moving targets like cricket balls and how our effector systems allow us to accurately hit, catch and hurl them. I am grateful to Gus for taking the first step, that the mind is an incredible information processing device. I know only a little more than nearly everyone else about how the mind works, but it gives me a considerable advantage in appreciating the complexity of human thought processes, even without anyone knowing the precise details. Get this concept right and one should then eschew unfortunately popular espousals of folk psychology, for example, about batsmen being instinctive or acting automatically. An idea to improve cricket commentary, I think.

In 'Watching Cricket on the Radio' I'm not asking, or necessarily expecting, people to agree with me. In any case, some of my ideas are silly, for effect and

[52] In pre-computer days, the Department of Experimental Psychology at the University of Cambridge developed a set of brass bells of various sizes and with each tuned to resonate at a particularly frequency. These could then be used in a way similar to how the ear works to decompose sounds into their component frequencies.

entertainment, which I cynically see as the worm on my educational hook. If I can get people to think a bit better, a bit more clearly, to make fewer goofs and be less lazy in thought, word and deed, then I shall be more than satisfied. If there were changes, for the better, to the business of cricket, how it is played and, particularly from this book, how it is presented by the sport's entertainment industries, then that would be brilliant, my cup would run over, and I might be tempted to come back for a second run.

Writing is hard work so I suppose it is perverse pleasure that I've done so much of it during my lifetime. Adding an entertainment factor has been my novel challenge with this book. I do hope my readers enjoy it. If it gives some people a few hours of surcease from less esoteric cares; if it causes consideration and reflection on matters concerning cricket; and if in future even one cricket commentator on the radio can keep reminding me whether the batsmen are right or left handed, then I should be satisfied[53].

---

[53] Should, shall, or will, we'll see.

Index

N.B. Main chapter topics in **bold**. End of chapter references in *italic*.

Lightning Source UK Ltd.
Milton Keynes UK
UKOW02f0826040416

271488UK00004B/296/P